THE COMPLETE GREEK TRAGEDIES

Edited by David Grene & Richmond Lattimore

THIRD EDITION *Edited by Mark Griffith & Glenn W. Most*

SOPHOCLES I

ANTIGONE *Translated by Elizabeth Wyckoff*

OEDIPUS THE KING *Translated by David Grene*

OEDIPUS AT COLONUS *Translated by Robert Fitzgerald*

The University of Chicago Press CHICAGO & LONDON

MARK GRIFFITH is professor of classics and of theater, dance, and performance studies at the University of California, Berkeley.

GLENN W. MOST is professor of ancient Greek at the Scuola Normale Superiore at Pisa and a visiting member of the Committee on Social Thought at the University of Chicago.

DAVID GRENE (1913–2002) taught classics for many years at the University of Chicago.

RICHMOND LATTIMORE (1906–1984), professor of Greek at Bryn Mawr College, was a poet and translator best known for his translations of the Greek classics, especially his versions of the *Iliad* and the *Odyssey*.

The University of Chicago Press, Chicago 60637
The University of Chicago Press, Ltd., London
© 2013 by The University of Chicago

25 24 23 22   10 11 12

ISBN-13: 978-0-226-31150-0 (cloth)
ISBN-13: 978-0-226-31151-7 (paper)
ISBN-13: 978-0-226-31153-1 (e-book)
ISBN-10: 0-226-31150-3 (cloth)
ISBN-10: 0-226-31151-1 (paper)
ISBN-10: 0-226-31153-8 (e-book)

Library of Congress Cataloging-in-Publication Data
Sophocles.
[Works. Selections. English]
Sophocles. — Third edition / edited by Mark Griffith and Glenn W. Most.
volumes. cm. — (The complete Greek tragedies)
ISBN 978-0-226-31150-0 (v. 1 : cloth : alk. paper) — ISBN 978-0-226-31151-7 (v. 1 : pbk. : alk. paper) — ISBN 978-0-226-31153-1 (v. 1 : e-book) — ISBN 978-0-226-31154-8 (v. 2 : cloth : alk. paper) — ISBN 978-0-226-31155-5 (v. 2 : pbk. : alk. paper) — ISBN 978-0-226-31156-2 (v. 2 : e-book) 1. Sophocles—Translations into English. 2. Greek drama (Tragedy)—Translations into English. 3. Mythology, Greek—Drama. I. Wyckoff, Elizabeth, 1915– II. Grene, David. III. Fitzgerald, Robert, 1910–1985. IV. Griffith, Mark (Classicist) V. Most, Glenn W. VI. Title. VII. Series: Complete Greek tragedies (Unnumbered)
   PA4414.A1G7 2013
   882'.01—dc23

                                    2012043847

♾ This paper meets the requirements of ANSI/NISO Z39.48-1992 (Permanence of Paper).

CONTENTS

EDITORS' PREFACE TO THE THIRD EDITION

The first edition of the *Complete Greek Tragedies*, edited by David Grene and Richmond Lattimore, was published by the University of Chicago Press starting in 1953. But the origins of the series go back even further. David Grene had already published his translation of three of the tragedies with the same press in 1942, and some of the other translations that eventually formed part of the Chicago series had appeared even earlier. A second edition of the series, with new translations of several plays and other changes, was published in 1991. For well over six decades, these translations have proved to be extraordinarily popular and resilient, thanks to their combination of accuracy, poetic immediacy, and clarity of presentation. They have guided hundreds of thousands of teachers, students, and other readers toward a reliable understanding of the surviving masterpieces of the three great Athenian tragedians: Aeschylus, Sophocles, and Euripides.

But the world changes, perhaps never more rapidly than in the past half century, and whatever outlasts the day of its appearance must eventually come to terms with circumstances very different from those that prevailed at its inception. During this same period, scholarly understanding of Greek tragedy has undergone significant development, and there have been marked changes not only in the readers to whom this series is addressed, but also in the ways in which these texts are taught and studied in universities. These changes have prompted the University of Chicago Press to perform another, more systematic revision of the translations, and we are honored to have been entrusted with this delicate and important task.

Our aim in this third edition has been to preserve and strengthen as far as possible all those features that have made the Chicago translations successful for such a long time, while at the same time revising the texts carefully and tactfully to bring them up to date and equipping them with various kinds of subsidiary help, so they may continue to serve new generations of readers.

Our revisions have addressed the following issues:

- Wherever possible, we have kept the existing translations. But we have revised them where we found this to be necessary in order to bring them closer to the ancient Greek of the original texts or to replace an English idiom that has by now become antiquated or obscure. At the same time we have done our utmost to respect the original translator's individual style and meter.

- In a few cases, we have decided to substitute entirely new translations for the ones that were published in earlier editions of the series. Euripides' *Medea* has been newly translated by Oliver Taplin, *The Children of Heracles* by Mark Griffith, *Andromache* by Deborah Roberts, and *Iphigenia among the Taurians* by Anne Carson. We have also, in the case of Aeschylus, added translations and brief discussions of the fragments of lost plays that originally belonged to connected tetralogies along with the surviving tragedies, since awareness of these other lost plays is often crucial to the interpretation of the surviving ones. And in the case of Sophocles, we have included a translation of the substantial fragmentary remains of one of his satyr-dramas, *The Trackers* (*Ichneutai*). (See "How the Plays Were Originally Staged" below for explanation of "tetralogy," "satyr-drama," and other terms.)

- We have altered the distribution of the plays among the various volumes in order to reflect the chronological order in which they were written, when this is known or can be estimated with some probability. Thus the *Oresteia* appears now as volume 2 of Aeschylus' tragedies, and the sequence of Euripides' plays has been rearranged.

- We have rewritten the stage directions to make them more consistent throughout, keeping in mind current scholarly understanding of how Greek tragedies were staged in the fifth century BCE. In general, we have refrained from extensive stage directions of an interpretive kind, since these are necessarily speculative and modern scholars often disagree greatly about them. The Greek manuscripts themselves contain no stage directions at all.

- We have indicated certain fundamental differences in the meters and modes of delivery of all the verse of these plays. Spoken language (a kind of heightened ordinary speech, usually in the iambic trimeter rhythm) in which the characters of tragedy regularly engage in dialogue and monologue is printed in ordinary Roman font; the sung verse of choral and individual lyric odes (using a large variety of different meters), and the chanted verse recited by the chorus or individual characters (always using the anapestic meter), are rendered in *italics*, with parentheses added where necessary to indicate whether the passage is sung or chanted. In this way, readers will be able to tell at a glance how the playwright intended a given passage to be delivered in the theater, and how these shifting dynamics of poetic register contribute to the overall dramatic effect.

- All the Greek tragedies that survive alternate scenes of action or dialogue, in which individual actors speak all the lines, with formal songs performed by the chorus. Occasionally individual characters sing formal songs too, or they and the chorus may alternate lyrics and spoken verse within the same scene. Most of the formal songs are structured as a series of pairs of stanzas of which the metrical form of the first one ("strophe") is repeated exactly by a second one ("antistrophe"). Thus the metrical structure will be, e.g., strophe A, antistrophe A, strophe B, antistrophe B, with each pair of stanzas consisting of a different sequence of rhythms. Occasionally a short stanza in a different metrical form ("mesode") is inserted in the middle between one strophe and the corresponding antistrophe, and sometimes the end of the whole series is marked with a single stanza in a different metrical form ("epode")—thus, e.g., strophe A, mesode, antistrophe A; or strophe A, antistrophe A, strophe B, antistrophe B, epode. We have indicated these metrical structures by inserting the terms

STROPHE, ANTISTROPHE, MESODE, and EPODE above the first line of the relevant stanzas so that readers can easily recognize the compositional structure of these songs.

- In each play we have indicated by the symbol ° those lines or words for which there are significant uncertainties regarding the transmitted text, and we have explained as simply as possible in textual notes at the end of the volume just what the nature and degree of those uncertainties are. These notes are not at all intended to provide anything like a full scholarly apparatus of textual variants, but instead to make readers aware of places where the text transmitted by the manuscripts may not exactly reflect the poet's own words, or where the interpretation of those words is seriously in doubt.
- For each play we have provided a brief introduction that gives essential information about the first production of the tragedy, the mythical or historical background of its plot, and its reception in antiquity and thereafter.
- For each of the three great tragedians we have provided an introduction to his life and work. It is reproduced at the beginning of each volume containing his tragedies.
- We have also provided at the end of each volume a glossary explaining the names of all persons and geographical features that are mentioned in any of the plays in that volume.

It is our hope that our work will help ensure that these translations continue to delight, to move, to astonish, to disturb, and to instruct many new readers in coming generations.

MARK GRIFFITH, *Berkeley*
GLENN W. MOST, *Florence*

INTRODUCTION TO SOPHOCLES

Sophocles was born in about 495 BCE, into a wealthy family from the deme of Colonus, close to the city center of Athens. He was thus about thirty years younger than Aeschylus (who died in 455), and about ten or fifteen years older than Euripides (who died just a few months before Sophocles, in 405).

In addition to being the most successful tragedian of his time, Sophocles was active in Athenian public life: he was appointed a treasurer (*hellenotamias*) in 443-42, elected a general (*strategos*) in 441-40 along with Pericles, and perhaps again in the 420s with Nicias; and he was selected to be a special magistrate (*proboulos*) during the emergency administration of 412-11, all of this in marked contrast to the apolitical life of Euripides. There was also an ancient tradition (perhaps apocryphal) that when the cult of the healing god Asclepius was first brought to Athens, it was for a while located in Sophocles' house.

Although we know for certain few details of Sophocles' personal life, he apparently had at least one son, Iophon, by his wife Nicostrate, and another, Ariston, by his mistress Theoris. Ariston's son was in turn named Sophocles, and both Iophon and Sophocles Jr. became successful tragedians. Among his friends were such luminaries as Herodotus, Pericles, and Ion of Chios, and he was said to be sociable and a "good-natured" man. He had a reputation for being something of a flirt and bisexual playboy. Stories that were later told of the octogenarian Sophocles' legal feuds with his sons may have been triggered by his depiction of fierce, lonely, embittered men in his plays (Ajax, Philoctetes,

Teiresias, and especially Oedipus cursing his son in *Oedipus at Colonus*).

Sophocles' career as a dramatist was long, prolific, and immensely successful. His first production in the annual tragedy competition at Athens was in 468 BCE. The plays he entered are not known, but they resulted in a victory over Aeschylus. Sophocles was still composing plays right up to his death in 405 (*Philoctetes*, produced in 409; *Oedipus at Colonus*, produced posthumously in 401).

Ancient sources knew the titles of 120 plays by Sophocles, which should mean thirty groups of four for the annual competition, each comprising three tragedies and a satyr-play. It is recorded that he won eighteen victories (thus even outdoing Aeschylus' thirteen, and far more than Euripides' five), and that he was never ranked lower than second in the competition. Unlike Aeschylus, Sophocles never composed a connected trilogy, that is, a sequence of plays performed together that focused on the same characters or family (like, for example, the *Oresteia*). Unfortunately we do not know what principles he may have used in designing each set of four plays in any given year. All of the seven plays we possess seem to have been performed in different years, and we do not even know the titles of any of the lost plays that accompanied them. As far as we can tell, however, each play was intended to be treated as a separate masterpiece—fully intelligible and self-contained on its own terms.

Any attempt to trace a development in Sophocles' style or worldview during his long career is hampered not only by the loss of all but seven of his plays, but also by the uncertain dating of several of the ones we do have. Sophocles' tragedies rarely contain references to actual current events or issues, and they rarely elicited parodies from Aristophanes (as several of Euripides' did). For only two Sophoclean plays do we possess definite information about their date of production, based on the original fifth-century festival competition records: *Philoctetes* (409) and *Oedipus at Colonus* (405/401). There is good external evidence for dating *Antigone* to 442 or 441, but for the other four plays we have to rely on stylistic—hence subjective—criteria. Most scholars nowadays are inclined to date *Ajax* and *The Women of Trachis* quite early (to the 460s-440s). *Electra* is probably late (perhaps 415-10). The date of *Oedipus the King* is uncertain, though many would like to place it in the early 420s because of its vivid depiction of plague—not a compelling argument.

Sophocles inherited from Aeschylus and the other early tragedians a well-established set of dramatic conventions and formal structures, and he does not appear to have made radical innovations of his own, except perhaps in the musical aspects, since he is credited with being the first Athenian playwright to introduce "Phrygian" and "Lydian" scales into the melodies of his lyrics. (None of this music survives.) Ancient critics disagreed as to whether it was Aeschylus or Sophocles who first employed a third speaking actor—earlier the rule had been that only two were allowed. Aristotle says that Sophocles was first, and that he also introduced scene-painting. In general, however, it was Euripides, along with his younger contemporary Agathon, who were generally regarded as the chief iconoclasts and experimenters in artistic forms and subject matter. Sophocles' gifts lay rather in refining and elaborating the possibilities of the tragic form: tightly constructed plots, more complex dialogue scenes, exploration of extreme emotional states and character contrasts, the subtle interweaving of spoken and musical elements, and an extraordinary richness and fluidity of verbal expression that is often very difficult to capture in English translation. To Aristotle in the fourth century, as to many lovers of drama since, Sophocles' plays appear to represent the pinnacle of what Greek tragedy was capable of achieving, the fulfilment of its very "nature."

After Sophocles died, his plays continued for centuries to be widely read and (presumably) performed all over the Greek-speaking world. A more or less complete collection of his plays was made in Alexandria during the third century BCE, though this no longer exists. Hundreds of fragments from his lost plays are found in quotations by other authors and in anthologies, and while he was never as widely read or imitated as Euripides or Menander (let alone Homer), Sophocles remained a classic both in the ancient schools and among later practitioners of the dramatic arts (including Ennius, Accius, and Pacuvius; Seneca; Corneille and Racine). The seven plays we possess today were probably selected in the second century CE, and from that point gradually the other plays ceased to be copied, and thus eventually were lost to posterity. At Byzantium (Constantinople, now Istanbul), three plays in particular were most widely copied: the "triad" of *Ajax*, *Electra*, and *Oedipus the King*. But the rest were never as close to extinction as the tragedies of Aeschylus, whose difficult style and more old-fashioned dramaturgy made his works less appealing to later readers.

A large papyrus unearthed at Oxyrhynchus (first published in 1912) contains a substantial chunk of the previously lost satyr-play titled *The Trackers* (*Ichneutai*), which is included in translation in this new edition of the Chicago Greek tragedies. Further papyrus finds have continued to add important scraps to our knowledge both of Sophocles' tragedies and of his satyr-dramas. But for the most part, even though we know that, for example, his *Phaedra* was influential and popular throughout antiquity, as were *Polyxena*, *Thyestes*, *Tereus* (about Procne and Philomela), *Inachus* (a satyr-play about Zeus and Io), and numerous other lost plays, Sophocles' reputation in the modern era has rested almost entirely on the seven plays that survive in medieval manuscripts. Of these, *Oedipus the King*, *Antigone*, and *Electra* have always been the most widely read and often staged, but all seven have been central to the discussions of theater historians, philosophers, and theorists of tragedy, and all of them have provoked adaptations, paintings, and translations in abundance, all over the world. Indeed, since the late eighteenth century, for many critics and philosophers it has been Sophocles' plays—along with Shakespeare's—that have been taken to represent the culmination of the genre of tragedy and its capacity to represent human experience and heroic suffering.

INTRODUCTION TO THE THEBAN PLAYS

Unlike Aeschylus' *Oresteia* and the trilogy that included his *Seven against Thebes*, the three Sophoclean plays we possess that deal with the family of Oedipus were not written to be performed together. Indeed, they seem to have been composed over several decades. *Antigone* was probably first performed in 442 or 441. The date of *Oedipus the King* is quite uncertain, though often surmised as being in the 420s. *Oedipus at Colonus* was produced posthumously by Sophocles' son in 401. The three plays occasionally disagree with one another in factual details, and in several passages of *Oedipus at Colonus* the hero is found correcting or critiquing ideas that had been propounded in the earlier *Oedipus the King*. Nonetheless, there are many respects in which the three plays speak to one another and convey a consistent portrayal of this family's terrible history, so it makes sense to consider them together in this introduction, even while it must be emphasized again that this is not a "trilogy" in the proper sense of that term.

The Myth

The story of the doomed descendants of King Labdacus of Thebes—Laius, Oedipus, and the sons of Oedipus, Eteocles and Polyneices—was extremely well known and often recounted in early Greek literature. The saga rivaled that of the Trojan War in popularity and significance, and various parts of it were narrated in epic poems (including the *Thebais* and the *Oedipodeia*, both now lost) attributed to Homer or one of his successors. It was also taken up in many lyric poems (including one by Stesichorus, of which fragments survive on papyrus). There were, of course, many different versions of the whole story, but the main outlines remain fairly consistent: King Laius and his wife, Jocasta (sometimes she has a different name), are informed by the oracle of Apollo that if she conceives and bears a son, he will grow up to kill his father and marry his mother. They do proceed to have a baby son, however, whom (in Sophocles' version, at least) they leave on a deserted hillside to die. He is rescued by a shepherd, and adopted by King Polybus of Corinth and his wife, Merope. The boy, named Oedipus, grows up believing himself to be Polybus' son and heir.

In due course, Oedipus encounters his real father at a crossroads, though neither recognizes the other. They fight and Oedipus kills Laius. He then comes to Thebes, which is being terrorized by the monstrous Sphinx. Oedipus solves the Sphinx's riddle and is hailed as the new king by the Thebans, which entails marrying the widow of the recently deceased king, Laius—she is, of course, his mother. In Sophocles' version of the story Oedipus and Jocasta have four children: two boys, Polyneices and Eteocles, and two girls, Antigone and Ismene. Eventually, the truth about Oedipus' identity (and the parricide and incest) is discovered.

What happens next varies from version to version. In some, Jocasta commits suicide, in others not. In some Oedipus continues to be the king of Thebes, in others, he either goes into exile or is deposed from the throne but remains in Thebes; in some, he blinds himself. It is not known when this detail of self-blinding was invented: it may have been Sophocles' innovation, though there seem to be hints of it in Aeschylus' (earlier) *Seven against Thebes*.

The ghastly problems continue into the next generation, with Oedipus' two sons quarreling violently about the succession. (In some versions of the story, Oedipus is still alive; in others he has already died.) Again, different versions account differently for this quarrel and its consequences; but in all of them Polyneices goes to live for a while in Argos, marries the daughter of the Argive king, Adrastus, and persuades the Argives to provide him with an army, with the intention of regaining the Theban throne by force. He and six other champions (the "Seven against Thebes") attack the city at its seven gates, while Eteocles organizes its defense. In the battle, the two brothers meet face to face and kill one another. Still, the defenders are victorious and the city is not captured.

Creon, Jocasta's brother and a leading military commander and former advisor to Oedipus, takes over as ruler. He decides to give honorific burial to Eteocles, but denies it to Polyneices (and in most versions, he denies burial also to the Argive dead). A dispute arises over the matter: in some versions (for example, in Euripides' *Suppliant Women*) the Athenians send an army to help the Argives defeat Creon and force the Thebans to surrender the Argive dead for proper burial. Sophocles seems to be innovating in *Antigone* by having only the corpse of Polyneices be the object of dispute, with the dead man's sister, Antigone, being the one who is resisting Creon and demanding the burial.

Where Oedipus was finally laid to rest seems to have been quite open-ended. Other elements in the story too, such as the role of Ismene or the possible intervention of Teiresias at one point or another, were handled quite differently by various authors, as was the issue of Apollo's oracle and its possible significance.

Of the surviving thirty-two Greek tragedies, no fewer than six are based on this Theban saga: apart from these three plays of Sophocles, we have Aeschylus' *Seven against Thebes* and Euripides' *Suppliant Women* and *Phoenician Women*. In addition, we know of numerous lost tragedies that dealt with this myth, including an *Antigone* and an *Oedipus* by Euripides and the two other plays of the Theban trilogy by Aeschylus (*Laius* and *Oedipus*).

Antigone

Sophocles is reported to have won first prize with his production of *Antigone* (probably in 442 or 441 BCE). We do not know the names of the other three plays that he presented that year. The play's considerable success and popularity seem to have influenced other writers and theater-makers profoundly, to the extent that Aeschylus' *Seven against Thebes* (first produced in 467) was extensively re-vised—some decades after its author's death—to make the final scenes follow the same dramatic course as Sophocles' play.

The idea of building a tragic plot around the bold and defiant resistance of Oedipus' daughter to Creon's authority, out of loy-alty to her brother, seems to have originated with this play. In-deed, Antigone as a character may herself have been Sophocles' invention. (By contrast, Ismene, the other daughter, who is a more cautious and conventionally minded foil to her extraordi-nary sister in this play, had a more significant role in previous versions of the story.) Likewise, the theme of Haemon's (Creon's son's) betrothal to one of Oedipus' daughters may have been an innovation, together with the concentration on the internal family conflict concerning the burial of the two brothers, rather than on the Argive demand that their soldiers be properly bur-ied. Haemon's suicide, and that of Creon's wife Eurydice, as well as Teiresias' intervention and warnings, are also probably new twists introduced by Sophocles—all of them serving to highlight the shocking downfall and misery of Creon.

In Sophocles' strikingly original play, the collision between the two major characters, Antigone and Creon, and the principles that each of them asserts has captured the imaginations of audi-ences, critics, and philosophers through the centuries. We may note that it is unusual for Sophocles to have a male chorus when his chief character is female; Antigone's isolation is thereby much enhanced, while the audience's sympathies, like the cho-rus', end up being divided between them.

The play seems to have been quite frequently performed in the fourth century and later, though direct evidence for this is slim, and it was clearly not as popular as Euripides' *Phoenician Women*, whose plot covered some of the same material (in a very different way). Euripides' *Antigone* (now lost) was also well known, and quite different. Although we know little about its date or con-tents, it appears that Antigone did not die in Euripides' version, but married Haemon and had a son with him. Representations of scenes from our play in ancient art are few. But *Antigone* eventually became one of the seven Sophoclean plays that were selected for standard school use in antiquity, and thus survived into the Byzantine era. About a dozen medieval manuscripts contain the play.

During the Middle Ages and early Renaissance, it was the Latin *Thebais* by Statius and the (incomplete) *Phoenician Women* by Seneca that were best known; and these are the basis for Boccaccio in his *De claris mulieribus* (*On Famous Women*). Since the eighteenth century, however, it has been above all Sophocles' treatment of Antigone, along with his two *Oedipus* plays, that have come to eclipse all others. Poems, letters, and essays by Shelley, De Quincey, Goethe, and many others were devoted to Antigone, and she was constantly depicted as the embodiment of virginal purity, sisterly love, and self-sacrifice. Especially notable are Hölderlin's translation of the play (1804), the opera by Mendelssohn (1841), and essays by Matthew Arnold (1849), George Eliot (1856), and Søren Kierkegaard (1843, and elsewhere), along with the lectures of G. W. F. Hegel (1818–1835).

In the twentieth and twenty-first centuries, writers, performers, critics, political scientists, and philosophers have continued to turn to Sophocles' heroine as a model of individual resistance to totalitarian rule, and/or as a martyr to the cause of family, or religion, or women's rights: for example, the composers Arthur Honegger (1927) and Carl Orff (1949), and playwright Bertolt Brecht (1947). Jean Anouilh's drama *Antigone* (1944) and Athol Fugard's *The Island* (1973) offer contrasting but equally brilliant variations on Sophocles' original; likewise the psychoanalyst Jacques Lacan (1959) and the philosopher Judith Butler (2000). Meanwhile Sophocles' play itself continues to stand out as one of the three or four most widely performed, read, discussed, and admired of all Greek tragedies.

Oedipus the King

When the play was composed and first performed is unknown. Many scholars have suggested the mid-420s because of the portrayal of the plague, but there is little evidence to support this or any other date. We are informed that Sophocles did not win first prize with *Oedipus the King*, but we do not know which other plays he presented with it, so the failure may not have been the result of the audience's dislike of this play in particular. Certainly we have plenty of evidence that the play did not take long to establish itself as one of Sophocles' best known and most admired.

The title of the play in antiquity was *Oedipus Tyrannos*, a designation signaling that Oedipus' position as ruler of Thebes was not inherited but came to him through some other kind of intervention or invitation: the word *tyrannos* did not necessarily carry pejorative associations (though it often did). We do not know who first attached this label to the play, or why—it may not have occurred until after the composition of *Oedipus at Colonus*, when scholars and commentators would have needed to distinguish the two. In Latin, the play has always been titled *Oedipus Rex*.

As previously noted, the broad outline of the story of Oedipus' fateful birth, unwitting parricide and incest, and ultimate self-discovery, was already well known by the time Sophocles wrote his play. In the modern era, his version has become the standard one, and there is a tendency to see this version as simply the way "the myth" goes. But a number of elements in Sophocles' plot were probably new and perhaps unexpected to the original audience. Certainly such details as the utterances of Apollo's oracle and the involvement of Teiresias, the Corinthian messenger, and the herdsman—all of them crucial to the action—are new.

But Sophocles' most distinctive innovations seem to have consisted—as Aristotle emphasizes in the *Poetics*—in his brilliant organization of the material so as to emphasize the elements of ignorance, irony, and unexpected recognition of the truth. The tragic effect of the play depends heavily on the fact that most of the crucial events occurred in the past, and that the audience knows or suspects much more than any individual character does (except possibly Teiresias). This is most strikingly true of Oedipus' edict stating that he will track down and exile the unknown killer of Laius; but it applies also to the announcement of the death of King Polybus of Corinth, Oedipus' supposed father. Throughout the play, it is the paradoxical—improbable, yet inevitable—process of struggling to recognize (or avoid recognizing) who is really who and what each character has already done, generally with the best of motives but terrible results, that causes Oedipus, Jocasta, and everyone else such intolerable anguish and that triggers in the audience such extraordinarily mixed feelings. This tragic tension is enhanced by the oracles of Apollo and warnings of Teiresias, by the chorus' songs of speculation and (mistaken) joy, by Jocasta's dismissal of the value of oracles, by the reports from the Corinthian messenger and the old herdsman, and above all by Oedipus' own determined pursuit of the city's salvation and the truth about himself.

The play was widely known and read throughout antiquity. Because so many other playwrights, including Aeschylus and Euripides, also composed Oedipus plays that do not survive, it is impossible to judge precisely how much the Sophocles version influenced subsequent writers. But Seneca's *Oedipus*, which had the most impact during the Renaissance, was certainly modeled on Sophocles', even while it also contains several major differences. In Byzantine times, Sophocles' play was frequently copied, so that almost two hundred manuscripts exist, most of them virtual duplicates of one another. Ever since the Renaissance, versions by Corneille (1658), Dryden and Lee (1678), Voltaire (1718), and more recently Stravinsky-Cocteau (1927; spectacularly staged by Julie Taymor in 1993), Gide (1931), and Pasolini (1967) constitute only a few of the most conspicuous examples, out of hundreds of productions and adaptations.

Sigmund Freud's exploration of the "Oedipus complex" as one of the cornerstones of his psychoanalytic theory of course added to the play's popular appeal, and it has remained the best known of all Greek tragedies throughout the twentieth and twenty-first centuries. But other interpretations of the play too, in which a not entirely guilty hero (a scapegoat) suffers so that the community can be saved, or a culture hero dies ("winter") to ensure the rebirth of vegetation and prosperity ("spring"), have also kept *Oedi-*

pus the King enduringly in the forefront of theatrical and philosophical attention. So too has the use of Oedipus as a metaphor for every human being's quest for personal identity and self-knowledge in a world full of ignorance and hidden horrors—perhaps even one ruled by divine indifference or malevolent fate. If there is one work that is regarded as most typically reflecting the Greeks' fatalistic or pessimistic outlook, this is probably it. Yet, as Aristotle observed, this is also a play whose astonishingly elegant and intricate construction makes it uniquely satisfying and pleasurable to contemplate.

Oedipus at Colonus

This play was written late in Sophocles' life. It was not performed until after his death, when his son Iophon presented it for the dramatic competition in 401. Ancient and modern critics have observed that a striking analogy exists between ancient anecdotes about the elderly Sophocles being engaged in a bitter dispute with his son and the dramatic scene of furious confrontation between Oedipus and Polyneices. But we cannot tell which may have influenced which.

The plot of this play seems to have been distinctly new with Sophocles. Various Greek authors before him had handled the later years and death of Oedipus in very different ways. In Homer Oedipus remains ruling in Thebes even after his parricide and incest are discovered. In Euripides' *Phoenician Women* (411–409 BC), Oedipus has abdicated but is still living in the palace while his sons take turns ruling Thebes. Even at the end of Sophocles' *Oedipus the King* it is not entirely clear whether or not he will go into exile, though that is his expressed wish and he is shown talking about it with his young daughters. In *Oedipus at Colonus* Sophocles continues along this trajectory, and we learn early in the play that Oedipus, now blind and weak, has been wandering for years from town to town as an outcast, attended only by Antigone. As the play proceeds, we learn that in Thebes his two sons, along with Creon, have refused to offer him shelter or support.

Only near the end of the play is Oedipus informed that an oracle has recently revealed that after his death he and his tomb will provide special protection to the community that harbors him, and that the Theban rulers therefore now wish to bring him back to die close to their borders. Innovations specific to this play include the intense focus on the Attic deme of Colonus (Sophocles' own home) as Oedipus' sanctuary and final resting place, the friendship and long-term alliance between Theseus as king of Athens and Oedipus, and the predictions of future defeats of Theban forces at Colonus thanks to the protection of Oedipus' spirit. Likewise the especially close relationship between Oedipus and his daughters, and the context of his cursing of Polyneices, seem distinctive and new. (In previous versions his curse had preceded and even caused the initial quarrel between the two sons.)

There are fewer signs that this play directly influenced later writers and audiences than there are for *Antigone* and *Oedipus the King*. But the play was included among Sophocles' select seven; and although it has not been extensively performed in the modern era, it has always commanded respect for its harrowing yet inspiring portrait of the long-suffering hero and his devoted daughters, as well as for the beauty of its lyrics. One modern oratorio adaptation, *The Gospel at Colonus* (by Lee Breuer and Bob Telson, 1989), based on Robert Fitzgerald's translation in our series, has been acclaimed by critics and audiences as a high point of twentieth-century adaptation of Greek tragedy.

HOW THE PLAYS WERE ORIGINALLY STAGED

Nearly all the plays composed by Aeschylus, Sophocles, and Euripides were first performed in the Theater of Dionysus at Athens, as part of the annual festival and competition in drama. This was not only a literary and musical event, but also an important religious and political ceremony for the Athenian community. Each year three tragedians were selected to compete, with each of them presenting four plays per day, a "tetralogy" of three tragedies and one satyr-play. The satyr-play was a type of drama similar to tragedy in being based on heroic myth and employing many of the same stylistic features, but distinguished by having a chorus of half-human, half-horse followers of Dionysus—sileni or satyrs—and by always ending happily. Extant examples of this genre are Euripides' *The Cyclops* (in *Euripides*, vol. 5) and Sophocles' *The Trackers* (partially preserved: in *Sophocles*, vol. 2).

The three competing tragedians were ranked by a panel of citizens functioning as amateur judges, and the winner received an honorific prize. Records of these competitions were maintained, allowing Aristotle and others later to compile lists of the dates when each of Aeschylus', Sophocles', and Euripides' plays were first performed and whether they placed first, second, or third in the competition (unfortunately we no longer possess the complete lists).

The tragedians competed on equal terms: each had at his disposal three actors (only two in Aeschylus' and in Euripides' earliest plays) who would often have to switch between roles as each play progressed, plus other nonspeaking actors to play attendants and other subsidiary characters; a chorus of twelve (in Aeschylus' time) or fifteen (for most of the careers of Sophocles and Eurip-ides), who would sing and dance formal songs and whose Cho-rus Leader would engage in dialogue with the characters or offer comment on the action; and a pipe-player, to accompany the sung portions of the play.

All the performers were men, and the actors and chorus mem-bers all wore masks. The association of masks with other Diony-sian rituals may have affected their use in the theater; but masks had certain practical advantages as well—for example, making it easy to play female characters and to change quickly between roles. In general, the use of masks also meant that ancient act-ing techniques must have been rather different from what we are used to seeing in the modern theater. Acting in a mask requires a more frontal and presentational style of performance toward the audience than is usual with unmasked, "realistic" acting; a masked actor must communicate far more by voice and stylized bodily gesture than by facial expression, and the gradual develop-ment of a character in the course of a play could hardly be indi-cated by changes in his or her mask. Unfortunately, however, we know almost nothing about the acting techniques of the Athe-nian theater. But we do know that the chorus members were all Athenian amateurs, and so were the actors up until the later part of the fifth century, by which point a prize for the best actor had been instituted in the tragic competition, and the art of acting (which of course included solo singing and dancing) was becom-ing increasingly professionalized.

The tragedian himself not only wrote the words for his play but also composed the music and choreography and directed the productions. It was said that Aeschylus also acted in his plays but that Sophocles chose not to, except early in his career, because his voice was too weak. Euripides is reported to have had a col-laborator who specialized in musical composition. The costs for each playwright's production were shared between an individual wealthy citizen, as a kind of "super-tax" requirement, and the city.

The Theater of Dionysus itself during most of the fifth cen-tury BCE probably consisted of a large rectangular or trapezoidal dance floor, backed by a one-story wooden building (the *skênê*), with a large central door that opened onto the dance floor. (Some scholars have argued that two doors were used, but the evidence is thin.) Between the *skênê* and the dance floor there may have been a narrow stage on which the characters acted and which communicated easily with the dance floor. For any particular play, the *skênê* might represent a palace, a house, a temple, or a cave, for example; the interior of this "building" was generally invisible to the audience, with all the action staged in front of it. Sophocles is said to have been the first to use painted scenery; this must have been fairly simple and easy to remove, as every play had a different setting. Playwrights did not include stage directions in their texts. Instead, a play's setting was indicated explicitly by the speaking characters.

All the plays were performed in the open air and in daylight. Spectators sat on wooden seats in rows, probably arranged in rectangular blocks along the curving slope of the Acropolis. (The stone semicircular remains of the Theater of Dionysus that are visible today in Athens belong to a later era.) Seating capacity seems to have been four to six thousand—thus a mass audience, but not quite on the scale of the theaters that came to be built during the fourth century BCE and later at Epidaurus, Ephesus, and many other locations all over the Mediterranean.

Alongside the *skênê*, on each side, there were passages through which actors could enter and exit. The acting area included the dance floor, the doorway, and the area immediately in front of the *skênê*. Occasionally an actor appeared on the roof or above it, as if flying. He was actually hanging from a crane (*mêchanê*: hence *deus ex machina*, "a god from the machine"). The *skênê* was also occasionally opened up—the mechanical details are uncertain—in order to show the audience what was concealed within (usually dead bodies). Announcements of entrances and exits, like the setting, were made by the characters. Although the medieval manuscripts of the surviving plays do not provide explicit stage directions, it is usually possible to infer from the words or from the context whether a particular entrance or exit is being made through a door (into the *skênê*) or by one of the side entrances. In later antiquity, there may have been a rule that one side entrance always led to the city center, the other to the countryside or harbor. Whether such a rule was ever observed in the fifth century is uncertain.

ANTIGONE

Translated by ELIZABETH WYCKOFF

ANTIGONE

Characters   ANTIGONE, daughter of Oedipus
    ISMENE, her sister
    CHORUS of Theban elders
    CREON, king of Thebes
    A GUARD
    HAEMON, son of Creon
    TEIRESIAS
    A MESSENGER
    EURYDICE, wife of Creon

Scene: Thebes, before the royal palace.

        (Antigone and Ismene enter from the palace.)

ANTIGONE
  My sister, my Ismene, do you know
  of any suffering from our father sprung
  that Zeus does not achieve for us survivors?
  There's nothing grievous, nothing full of doom,°
  or shameful, or dishonored, I've not seen: 5
  your sufferings and mine.
  And now, what of this edict which they say
  the commander has proclaimed to the whole people?
  Have you heard anything? Or don't you know
  that our enemies' trouble comes upon our friends?   10

ISMENE
  I've heard no word, Antigone, of our friends,

not sweet nor bitter, since that single moment
when we two lost two brothers
who died on one day by a double blow.
And since the Argive army went away   15
this very night, I have no further news
of fortune or disaster for myself.

ANTIGONE

I knew it well, and brought you from the house
for just this reason, that you alone may hear.

ISMENE

What is it? Clearly some news has clouded you.   20

ANTIGONE

It has indeed. Creon will give the one
of our two brothers honor in the tomb;
the other none. Eteocles, with just observance treated,
as law provides he has hidden under earth   25
to have full honor with the dead below.
But Polyneices' corpse who died in pain,
they say he has proclaimed to the whole town
that none may bury him and none bewail,
but leave him, unwept, untombed, a rich sweet sight
for the hungry birds' beholding and devouring.   30
        Such orders they say the worthy Creon gives
to you and me—yes, yes, I say to *me*—
and that he's coming to proclaim it clear
to those who know it not.
Further: he has the matter so at heart   35
that anyone who dares attempt the act
will die by public stoning in the town.
So there you have it and you soon will show
if you are noble, or worthless, despite your high birth.

ISMENE

If things have reached this stage, what can I do,
poor sister, that will help to make or mend?   40

ANTIGONE

Think, will you share my labor and my act?

ISMENE

What will you risk? And where is your intent?

ANTIGONE

Will you take up that corpse along with me?

ISMENE

To bury him you mean, when it's forbidden?

ANTIGONE

My brother, and yours, though you may wish he were not.° 45
I never shall be found to be his traitor.

ISMENE

O reckless one, when Creon spoke against it!

ANTIGONE

It's not for him to keep me from my own.

ISMENE

Alas. Remember, sister, how our father
perished abhorred, ill-famed: 50
himself with his own hand, through his own curse
destroyed both eyes.
Remember next his mother and his wife
finishing life in the shame of the twisted noose.
And third, two brothers on a single day, 55
poor creatures, murdering, a common doom
each with his arm accomplished on the other.
And now look at the two of us alone.
We'll perish terribly if we violate law
and try to cross the royal vote and power. 60
We must remember that we two are women,
so not to fight with men;
and that since we are subject to stronger power
we must hear these orders, or any that may be worse.

So I shall ask of them beneath the earth   65
forgiveness, for in these things I am forced,
and shall obey the men in power. I know
that wild and futile action makes no sense.

ANTIGONE
I wouldn't urge it. And if now you wished
to act, you wouldn't please me as a partner.   70
Be what you want to; but that man shall I
bury. For me, the doer, death is best.
Loving, I shall lie with him, yes, with my loved one,
when I have dared the crime of piety.
Longer the time in which to please the dead
than the time with those up here.   75
There shall I lie forever. You may see fit
to keep from honor what the gods have honored.

ISMENE
I shall do no dishonor. But to act
against the citizens, that's beyond my means.

ANTIGONE
That's your excuse. Now I go, to heap   80
the burial mound for him, my dearest brother.

ISMENE
Oh my poor sister. How I fear for you!

ANTIGONE
For me, don't worry. You clear your own fate.

ISMENE
At least give no one notice of this act;
you keep it hidden, and I'll do the same.   85

ANTIGONE
Dear gods! Denounce me. I shall hate you more
if silent, not proclaiming this to all.

ISMENE

You have a hot mind over chilly things.

ANTIGONE

I know I please those whom I most should please.

ISMENE

If but you can. You crave what can't be done.   90

ANTIGONE

And so, when strength runs out, I shall give over.

ISMENE

Wrong from the start, to chase what cannot be.

ANTIGONE

If that's your saying, I shall hate you first,
and next the dead will hate you in all justice.
But let me and my own ill counseling   95
suffer this terror. I shall suffer nothing
so great as to stop me dying with honor.

ISMENE

Go, since you want to. But know this: you go
senseless indeed, but loved by those who love you.

*(Exit Ismene into the palace. Exit Antigone to one
side. Enter the Chorus from the other side.)*

CHORUS [*singing*]

STROPHE A

*Sun's own radiance, fairest light ever shone on the seven gates of
Thebes,*   100
then did you shine, O golden day's
eye, coming over Dirce's stream,   105
on the man who had come from Argos with all his armor
running now in headlong fear as you shook his bridle free.

[*chanting*]
He was stirred by the dubious quarrel of Polyneices.   110

So, screaming shrill,
like an eagle over the land he flew,
covered with white-snow wing,
with many weapons,   115
with horse-hair crested helms.

ANTISTROPHE A [singing]

He who had stood above our halls, gaping about our seven gates,
with that circle of blood-thirsting spears:
gone, without our blood in his jaws,   120
before the torch took hold on our tower crown.
Rattle of war at his back; hard the fight for the dragon's foe.   125

[chanting]
The boasts of a proud tongue are for Zeus to hate.
So seeing them streaming on
in insolent clangor of gold,   130
he struck with hurling fire him who rushed
for the high wall's top,
hoping to yell out "victory."

STROPHE B [singing]

Swinging, striking the earth he fell
fire in hand, who in mad attack,   135
had raged against us with blasts of hate.
He failed. And differently from one to another
on both sides great Ares dealt his blows about,
first in our war team.   140

[chanting]
The captains assigned for seven gates
fought with our seven and left behind
their brazen arms as an offering
to Zeus who is turner of battle.
All but those two wretches, sons of one man,
one mother's sons, who planted their spears   145
each against each and found the share
of a common death together.

ANTISTROPHE B [*singing*]

Great-named Victory comes to us
answering Thebe's warrior joy.
Let us forget the wars just done   150
and visit the shrines of the gods,
all, with night-long dance which Bacchus will lead,
he who shakes Thebe's acres.

(Creon enters from the side.)

[*chanting*]

    Now here he comes, the king of the land,   155
    Creon, Menoeceus' son,
    newly appointed by the gods' new fate.
    What plan that beats about his mind
    has made him call this council session,   160
    sending his summons to all?

CREON

My friends, the very gods who shook the state
with mighty surge have set it straight again.
So now I sent for you, chosen from all,
first, because I knew you constant in respect   165
to Laius' royal power; and again
when Oedipus had set the state to rights,
and when he perished, you were faithful still
in mind to the descendants of the dead.
When they two perished by a double fate,   170
on one day struck and striking and defiled
each by each other's hand, now it comes that I
hold all the power and the royal throne
through close connection with the perished men.
    You cannot learn of any man the soul,   175
the mind, and the intent until he shows
his practice of the government and law.
For I believe that he who controls the state
if he holds not to the best plans of all,

but locks his tongue up through some kind of fear,   180
he is worst of all who are or were.
And he who counts another greater friend
than his own fatherland, I put him nowhere.
So I—may Zeus all-seeing always know it—
could not keep silent as disaster crept   185
upon the town, destroying hope of safety.
Nor could I count the enemy of the land
friend to myself, not I who know so well
that it's she, the land, who saves us, sailing straight,
and only so can we have friends at all.   190
      With such good rules shall I enlarge our state.
And now I have proclaimed their brother-edict.
In the matter of the sons of Oedipus,
citizens, know: Eteocles who died,
defending this our town with champion spear,   195
is to be covered in the grave and granted
all holy rites we give the noble dead.
But his brother Polyneices, whom I name
the exile who came back and sought to burn
his fatherland, the gods of his own kin,   200
who tried to gorge on blood he shared, and lead
the rest of us as slaves—
it is announced that no one in this town
may give him burial or mourn for him.
Leave him unburied, leave his corpse disgraced,   205
a dinner for the birds and for the dogs.
Such is my mind. Never shall I, myself,
honor the wicked and reject the just.
The man who is well-minded to the state
from me in death and life shall have his honor.   210

CHORUS LEADER
    This resolution, Creon, is your own,
    in the matter of the traitor and the true.

For you can make such rulings as you will
about the living and about the dead.

CREON

Now you be sentinels of the decree.   215

CHORUS LEADER

Order some younger man to take this on.

CREON

Already there are watchers of the corpse.

CHORUS LEADER

What other order would you give us, then?

CREON

Not to take sides with any who disobey.

CHORUS LEADER

No fool is fool to the point of loving death.   220

CREON

Death is the price. But often we have known
men to be ruined by the hope of profit.

(Enter, from the side, a Guard.)

GUARD

My lord, I cannot claim I'm out of breath
from rushing here with light and hasty step,
for I had many haltings in my thought   225
making me double back upon my road.
My mind kept saying many things to me:
"Why go where you will surely pay the price?"
"Fool, are you halting? And if Creon learns
from someone else, how shall you not be hurt?"   230
Turning this over, on I dillydallied.
And so a short trip turned itself to long.
Finally, though, my coming here won out.

If what I say is nothing, still I'll say it.
For I come clutching to one single hope   235
that I can't suffer what is not my fate.

CREON

What is it that brings on this gloom of yours?

GUARD

I want to tell you first about myself.
I didn't do it, didn't see who did it.
It isn't right for me to get in trouble.   240

CREON

Your aim is good. You fence the facts around.
It's clear you have some shocking news to tell.

GUARD

Terrible tidings make for long delays.

CREON

Speak out the story, and then get away.

GUARD

I'll tell you. Someone left the corpse just now,   245
burial all accomplished, thirsty dust
strewn on the flesh, the ritual complete.

CREON

What are you saying? What man has dared to do it?

GUARD

I wouldn't know. There were no marks of picks,
no grubbed-out earth. The ground was dry and hard,   250
no trace of wheels. The doer left no sign.
When the first fellow on the day-shift showed us,
we all were sick with wonder.
For he was hidden, not inside a tomb,   255
but light dust upon him, enough to avert pollution;
no wild beast's track, nor track of any hound
having been near, nor was the body torn.

We roared bad words about, guard against guard,   260
almost came to blows. No one was there to stop us.
Each man had done it, nobody had done it
so as to prove it on him—we couldn't tell.
We were prepared to hold to red-hot iron,
to walk through fire, to swear before the gods   265
we hadn't done it, hadn't shared the plan,
when it was plotted or when it was done.
And last, when all our sleuthing came out nowhere,
one fellow spoke, who made our heads to droop
low toward the ground. We couldn't disagree.   270
We couldn't see a chance of getting off.
He said we had to tell you all about it.
We couldn't hide the fact.
So he won out. The lot chose poor old me
to win the prize. So here I am unwilling,   275
quite sure you people hardly want to see me.
Nobody likes the bringer of bad news.

CHORUS LEADER
Lord, while he spoke, my mind kept on debating.
Isn't this action possibly a god's?

CREON
Stop now, before you fill me up with rage,   280
or you'll prove yourself insane as well as old.
Unbearable, your saying that the gods
take any kindly forethought for this corpse.
Would it be they had hidden him away,
honoring his good service, he who came   285
to burn their pillared temples and their wealth,
raze their land, and break apart their laws?
Or have you seen them honor wicked men?
It isn't so.
No, from the first there were some men in town   290
who took the edict hard, and growled against me,
who secretly were shaking their heads, not pulling

honestly in the yoke, no way my friends.
These are the people—oh it's clear to me—
who have bribed these men and brought about the deed. 295
No current standard among men's as bad
as silver currency. This destroys the state;
this drives men from their homes; this wicked teacher
drives solid citizens to acts of shame.
It shows men how to act as criminals 300
and know the deeds of utter unholiness.
But every hired hand who helped in this
has brought on himself the sentence he shall have.
    And further, as I still revere great Zeus,
understand this, I tell you under oath: 305
if you don't find the very man whose hands
buried the corpse and bring him for me to see,
not death alone shall be enough for you
till living, strung up, you make clear the crime.
For the future you'll have learned that profiteering 310
has its rules, and that it doesn't pay
to squeeze a profit out of every source.
For you'll have seen that more men come to doom
through dirty profits than are sustained by them.

GUARD
May I say something? Or just turn and go? 315

CREON
Aren't you aware your speech is most unwelcome?

GUARD
Does it annoy your ears, or your mind?

CREON
Why are you out to allocate my pain?

GUARD
The doer hurts your mind. I hurt your ears.

CREON

You are a quibbling rascal through and through.   320

GUARD

But anyhow I never did the deed.

CREON

And you the man who sold your life for money!

GUARD

Oh!
How terrible to guess, and guess at lies!

CREON

Go polish up your guesswork. If you don't
show me the doers you will have to say   325
that wicked payments work their own revenge.

GUARD

Indeed, I pray he's found, but yes or no,
taken or not as luck may settle it,
you won't see me returning to this place.
Saved when I neither hoped nor thought to be,   330
I owe the gods a mighty debt of thanks.

(*Exit Creon into the palace. Exit the Guard by the way he came.*)

CHORUS [*singing*]

STROPHE A

Many the wonders but nothing is stranger than man.
This thing crosses the sea in the winter's storm,   335
making his path through the roaring waves.
And she, the greatest of gods, the Earth—
ageless she is, and unwearied—he wears her away
as the ploughs go up and down from year to year   340
and his mules turn up the soil.

ANTISTROPHE A

Lighthearted nations of birds he snares and leads,

wild beast tribes and the salty brood of the sea,   345
with the twisted mesh of his nets, this clever man.
He controls with craft the beasts of the open air,
walkers on hills. The horse with his shaggy mane   350
he holds and harnesses, yoked about the neck,
and the strong bull of the mountain.

STROPHE B

Language, and thought like the wind
and the feelings that govern a city,   355
he has taught himself, and shelter against the cold,
refuge from rain. He can always help himself.
He faces no future helpless. There's only death
that he cannot find an escape from. He has contrived   360
refuge from illnesses once beyond all cure.

ANTISTROPHE B

Clever beyond all dreams
the inventive craft that he has   365
which may drive him one time to good or another to evil.
When he honors the laws of the land and the gods' sworn right
high indeed is his city; but cityless the man   370
who dares to dwell with dishonor. Not by my fireside,
never to share my thoughts, who does these things.   375

(Enter the Guard with Antigone, from the side.)

[Chorus now chanting]
My mind is split at this awful sight.
I know her. I cannot deny
Antigone is here.
Alas, the unhappy girl,
unhappy Oedipus' child.   380
Oh what is the meaning of this?
It cannot be you that they bring
for breaking the royal law,
caught in sheer madness.

GUARD

This is the woman who has done the deed.
We caught her at the burying. Where's the king?   385

(Enter Creon from the palace.)

CHORUS LEADER

Back from the house again just when he's needed.

CREON

What must I measure up to? What has happened?

GUARD

Lord, one should never swear off anything.
Afterthought makes the first resolve a liar.
I could have vowed I wouldn't come back here   390
after your threats, after the storm I faced.
But joy that comes beyond the wildest hope
is bigger than all other pleasure known.
I'm here, though I swore not to be, and bring   395
this girl. We caught her burying the dead.
This time we didn't need to shake the lots;
mine was the luck, all mine.
So now, lord, take her, you, and question her
and prove her as you will. But I am free.
And I deserve full clearance on this charge.   400

CREON

Explain the circumstance of the arrest.

GUARD

She was burying the man. You have it all.

CREON

Is this the truth? And do you grasp its meaning?

GUARD

I saw her burying the very corpse
you had forbidden. Is this adequate?   405

CREON

How was she caught and taken in the act?

GUARD

It was like this: when we got back again
struck with those dreadful threatenings of yours,
we swept away the dust that hid the corpse.   410
We stripped it back to slimy nakedness.
And then we sat to windward on the hill
so as to dodge the smell.
We poked each other up with growling threats
if anyone was careless of his work.
For some time this went on, till it was noon.   415
The sun was high and hot. Then from the earth
up rose a dusty whirlwind to the sky,
filling the plain, smearing the forest leaves,
clogging the upper air. We shut our eyes,   420
sat and endured the plague the gods had sent.
Then the storm left us after a long time.
We saw the girl. She cried the sharp and shrill
cry of a bitter bird which sees the nest
bare where the young birds lay.   425
So this same girl, seeing the body stripped,
cried with great groanings, called out dreadful curses
upon the people who had done the deed.
Soon in her hands she brought the thirsty dust,
and holding high a pitcher of wrought bronze   430
she poured the three libations for the dead.
We saw this and rushed down. We trapped her fast;
and she was calm. We taxed her with the deeds
both past and present. Nothing was denied.   435
And I was glad, and yet I took it hard.
One's own escape from trouble makes one glad;
but bringing friends to trouble is hard grief.
Still, I care less for all these second thoughts
than for the fact that I myself am safe.   440

CREON

You there, whose head is drooping to the ground,
do you admit this, or deny you did it?

ANTIGONE

I say I did it and I don't deny it.

CREON   (To the Guard.)

Take yourself off wherever you wish to go
free of a heavy charge.   445

                                               (To Antigone.)

You—tell me not at length but in a word.
You knew the order not to do this thing?

ANTIGONE

I knew—of course I knew. The word was plain.

CREON

And still you dared to overstep these laws?

ANTIGONE

For me it was not Zeus who made that order.   450
Nor did that Justice who lives with the gods below
mark out such laws to hold among mankind.
Nor did I think your orders were so strong
that you, a mortal man, could overrun
the gods' unwritten and unfailing laws.   455
Not now, nor yesterday's, they always live,
and no one knows their origin in time.
So not through fear of any man's proud spirit
would I be likely to neglect these laws,
and draw on myself the gods' sure punishment.
        I knew that I must die—how could I not?—   460
even without your edict. If I die
before my time, I say it is a gain.
Who lives in sorrows many as are mine
how shall he not be glad to gain his death?

And so, for me to meet this fate's no grief.   465
But if I left that corpse, my mother's son,
dead and unburied I'd have cause to grieve
as now I grieve not.
And if you think my acts are foolishness
the foolishness may be in a fool's eye.   470

CHORUS LEADER
   The girl is fierce. She's her father's child.
She cannot yield to trouble; nor could he.

CREON
   These rigid spirits are the first to fall.
The strongest iron, hardened in the fire,   475
most often ends in scraps and shatterings.
Small curbs bring raging horses back to terms:
enslaved to his neighbor, who can think of pride?
This girl was expert in her insolence   480
when she broke bounds beyond established law.
Once she had done it, insolence the second,
to boast her doing, and to laugh in it.
I am no man and she the man instead
if she can have this conquest without pain.   485
She is my sister's child, but were she child
of closer kin than any at my hearth,
she and her sister should not so escape
a dreadful death. I charge Ismene too.
She shared the planning of this burial.   490
Call her outside. I saw her in the house,
maddened, no longer mistress of herself.
The sly intent betrays itself sometimes
before the secret plotters work their wrong.
I hate it too when someone caught in crime   495
then wants to make it seem a lovely thing.

ANTIGONE
   Do you want more than my arrest and death?

CREON

No more than that. For that is all I need.

ANTIGONE

Why are you waiting? Nothing that you say
fits with my thought. I pray it never will.   500
Nor will you ever like to hear my words.
And yet what greater glory could I find
than giving my own brother funeral?
All these would say that they approved my act
did fear not mute them.   505
A king is fortunate in many ways,
and most, that he can act and speak at will.

CREON

None of these others see the case this way.

ANTIGONE

They see, and do not say. You have them cowed.

CREON

And you are not ashamed to think alone?   510

ANTIGONE

It is no shame to serve blood relatives.

CREON

Was not he who died on the other side your brother?

ANTIGONE

Full brother, on both sides, my parents' child.

CREON

Your act of grace, in his regard, is crime.

ANTIGONE

The corpse below would never say it was.   515

CREON

When you honor him and the criminal just alike?

ANTIGONE

It was a brother, not a slave, who died.

CREON

Died to destroy this land the other guarded.

ANTIGONE

Death yearns for equal law for all the dead.

CREON

Not that the good and bad draw equal shares.   520

ANTIGONE

Who knows but this is holiness below?

CREON

Never is the enemy, even in death, a friend.

ANTIGONE

I cannot share in hatred, but in love.

CREON

Then go down there, if you must love, and love
the dead. No woman rules me while I live.   525

(Ismene is brought from the palace under guard.)

CHORUS [*chanting*]

> *Look there! Ismene is coming out.*
> *She loves her sister and mourns,*
> *with clouded brow and bloodied cheeks,*
> *tears on her lovely face.*   530

CREON

You, lurking like a viper in the house,
who sucked me dry, while I raised unawares
a twin destruction planned against the throne.
Now tell me, do you say you shared this deed?
Or will you swear you didn't even know?   535

ISMENE

I did the deed if she agrees I did.
I am accessory and share the blame.

ANTIGONE

Justice will not allow this. You did not
wish for a part, nor did I give you one.

ISMENE

You are in trouble, and I'm not ashamed   540
to sail beside you into suffering.

ANTIGONE

Death and the dead, they know whose act it was.
I cannot love a friend whose love's mere words.

ISMENE

Sister, I pray, don't fence me out from honor,
from death with you, and honor done the dead.   545

ANTIGONE

Don't die along with me, nor make your own
that which you did not do. My death's enough.

ISMENE

When you are gone what life can I desire?

ANTIGONE

Love Creon. He's your kinsman and your care.

ISMENE

Why hurt me, when it does yourself no good?   550

ANTIGONE

I also suffer, when I laugh at you.

ISMENE

What further service can I do you now?

ANTIGONE

To save yourself. I shall not envy you.

ISMENE

    Alas for me. Am I outside your fate?

ANTIGONE

    Yes. For you chose to live when I chose death.   555

ISMENE

    At least I was not silent. You were warned.

ANTIGONE

    Some will have thought you wiser. Some will not.

ISMENE

    And yet the blame is equal for us both.

ANTIGONE

    Take heart. You live. My life died long ago.

    And that has made me fit to help the dead.   560

CREON

    One of these girls has shown her lack of sense

    just now. The other had it from her birth.

ISMENE

    Yes, king. When people fall in deep distress

    their native sense departs, and will not stay.

CREON

    You chose your mind's distraction when you chose   565

    to work out wickedness with this wicked girl.

ISMENE

    What life is there for me to live without her?

CREON

    Don't speak of her. For she is here no more.

ISMENE

    But will you kill your own son's promised bride?

CREON

    Oh, there are other furrows for his plough.

ISMENE

But where the closeness that has bound these two?   570

CREON

Not for my sons will I choose wicked wives.

ISMENE°

Dear Haemon, your father robs you of your rights.

CREON

You and your marriage trouble me too much.

ISMENE

You will take away his bride from your own son?

CREON

Yes. Death will help me break this marriage off.   575

CHORUS LEADER

It seems determined that the girl must die.

CREON

You helped determine it. Now, no delay!
Slaves, take them in. They must be women now.
No more free running.
Even the bold will flee when they see Death   580
drawing in close enough to end their life.

(Antigone and Ismene are taken inside.)

CHORUS [singing]

STROPHE A

Fortunate they whose lives have no taste of pain.
For those whose house is shaken by the gods   585
escape no kind of doom. It extends to all the kin
like the wave that comes when the winds of Thrace
run over the dark of the sea.
The black sand of the bottom is brought from the depth;   590
the beaten cliffs sound back with a hollow cry.

ANTISTROPHE A

Ancient the sorrow of Labdacus' house, I know.
Dead men's grief comes back, and falls on grief.   595
No generation can free the next.
One of the gods will strike. There is no escape.
So now the light goes out
for the house of Oedipus, while the bloody knife   600
cuts the remaining root,° in folly and the mind's fury.

STROPHE B

What transgression of man, O Zeus, can bind your power?
Not sleep can destroy it who governs all,°   606
nor the weariless months the gods have set. Unaged in time
monarch you rule in Olympus' gleaming light.   610
Near time, far future, and the past,
one law controls them all:
any greatness in human life brings doom.

ANTISTROPHE B

Wandering hope brings help to many men.
But others she tricks with giddy loves,   616
and her quarry knows nothing until he has walked into flame.
Word of wisdom it was when someone said,   620
"The bad looks like the good
to him a god would doom."
Only briefly is that one free from doom.   625

(Haemon enters from the side.)

[chanting]
            Here is Haemon, your one surviving son.
            Does he come in grief at the fate of his bride,
            in pain that he's tricked of his wedding?   630

CREON
    Soon we shall know more than a seer could tell us.
    Son, have you heard the vote condemned your bride?
    And are you here, maddened against your father,
    or are we friends, whatever I may do?

HAEMON

My father, I am yours. You keep me straight   635
with your good judgment, which I shall ever follow.
Nor shall a marriage count for more with me
than your kind leading.

CREON

There's my good boy. So should you hold at heart
and stand behind your father all the way.   640
It is for this men pray they may beget
households of dutiful obedient sons,
who share alike in punishing enemies,
and give due honor to their father's friends.
Whoever breeds a child that will not help,   645
what has he sown but trouble for himself,
and for his enemies laughter full and free?
Son, do not let your lust mislead your mind,
all for a woman's sake, for well you know
how cold the thing he takes into his arms   650
who has a wicked woman for his wife.
What deeper wound than a loved one who is evil?
Oh spit her forth forever, as your foe.
Let the girl marry somebody in Hades.
Since I have caught her in the open act,   655
the only one in town who disobeyed,
I shall not now proclaim myself a liar,
but kill her. Let her sing her song of Zeus
the guardian of blood kin.
If I allow disorder in my house
I'd surely have to license it abroad.   660
A man who deals in fairness with his own,
he can make manifest justice in the state.
But he who crosses law, or forces it,
or hopes to dictate orders to the rulers,
shall never have a word of praise from me.   665
The man the state has put in place must have

obedient hearing to his least command
when it is right, and even when it's not.
He who accepts this teaching I can trust,
ruler, or ruled, to function in his place,
to stand his ground even in the storm of spears, 670
a comrade to trust in battle at one's side.
There is no greater wrong than disobedience.
This ruins cities, this tears down our homes,
this breaks the battlefront in panic-rout.
If men live decently it is because
obedience saves their very lives for them. 675
So I must guard the men who yield to order,
not let myself be beaten by a woman.
Better, if it must happen, that a man
should overset me.
I won't be called weaker than womankind. 680

CHORUS LEADER
We think—unless our age is cheating us—
that what you say is sensible and right.

HAEMON
Father, the gods have given men good sense,
the highest and best possession that we have.
I couldn't find the words in which to claim 685
that there was error in your late remarks.
Yet someone else might bring some further light.
Because I am your son I must keep watch
on all men's doing where it touches you,
their speech, and most of all, their discontents.
Your presence frightens any common man 690
from saying things you would not care to hear.
But in dark corners I have heard them say
how the whole town is grieving for this girl,
unjustly doomed, if ever woman was,
to die in shame for glorious action done. 695
She would not leave her fallen, slaughtered brother

there, as he lay, unburied, for the birds
and hungry dogs to make an end of him.
Does she not truly deserve a golden prize?
This is the undercover speech in town.   700
        Father, your welfare is my greatest good.
What precious gift in life for any child
outweighs a father's fortune and good fame?
And so a father feels his children's faring.
So, do not have one mind, and one alone   705
that only your opinion can be right.
Whoever thinks that he alone is wise,
his eloquence, his mind, above the rest,
come the unfolding, it shows his emptiness.
A man, though wise, should never be ashamed   710
of learning more, and must not be too rigid.
Have you not seen the trees beside storm torrents—
the ones that bend preserve their limbs and leaves,
while the resistant perish root and branch?
And so the ship that will not slacken sail,   715
the ropes drawn tight, unyielding, overturns.
She ends the voyage with her keel on top.
No, yield your wrath, allow a change of stand.
Young as I am, if I may give advice,
I'd say it would be best if men were born   720
perfect in wisdom, but that failing this
(which often fails) it can be no dishonor
to learn from others when they speak good sense.

CHORUS LEADER
    Lord, if your son has spoken to the point
    you should take his lesson. He should do the same.   725
    Both sides have spoken well.

CREON
    At my age I'm to school my mind by his?
    This boy instructor is my master, then?

HAEMON

    I urge no wrong. I'm young, but you should watch
    my actions, not my years, to judge of me.

CREON

    A loyal action, to respect disorder?   730

HAEMON

    I wouldn't urge respect for wickedness.

CREON

    You don't think she is sick with that disease?

HAEMON

    Your fellow citizens maintain she's not.

CREON

    Is the town to tell me how I ought to rule?

HAEMON

    Now there you speak just like a boy yourself.   735

CREON

    Am I to rule by other mind than mine?

HAEMON

    No city is property of a single man.

CREON

    But custom gives possession to the ruler.

HAEMON

    You'd rule a desert beautifully alone.

CREON   *(To the Chorus.)*

    It seems he's firmly on the woman's side.   740

HAEMON

    If you're a woman. It is you I care for.

CREON

    Wicked, to try conclusions with your father.

HAEMON

When you conclude unjustly, so I must.

CREON

Am I unjust, when I respect my office?

HAEMON

You don't respect it, trampling down the gods' due.   745

CREON

Your mind is poisoned. Weaker than a woman!

HAEMON

At least you'll never see me yield to shame.

CREON

Your whole long argument is but for her.

HAEMON

And you, and me, and for the gods below.

CREON

As long as she lives, you shall not marry her.   750

HAEMON

Then she shall die—and her death will bring another.

CREON

Your boldness makes more progress. Threats, indeed!

HAEMON

No threat, to speak against your empty plan.

CREON

Past due, sharp lessons for your empty brain.

HAEMON

If you weren't father, I should call you mad.   755

CREON

Don't flatter me with "father," you woman's slave.

HAEMON

You wish to speak but never wish to hear.

CREON

You think so? By Olympus, you shall not
revile me with these tauntings and go free.
Bring out the hateful creature; she shall die   760
full in his sight, close at her bridegroom's side.

HAEMON

Not at my side! Don't think that! She will not
die next to me. And you yourself will not
ever lay eyes upon my face again.
Find other friends to rave with after this.   765

(Exit Haemon, to the side.)

CHORUS LEADER

Lord, he has gone with all the speed of rage.
When such a young man is grieved his mind is hard.

CREON

Oh, let him go, and plan superhuman action.
In any case the girls shall not escape.

CHORUS LEADER

You plan the punishment of death for both?   770

CREON

Not her who did not do it. You are right.

CHORUS LEADER

And what death have you chosen for the other?

CREON

To take her where the foot of man comes not.
There shall I hide her in a hollowed cave
living, and leave her just so much to eat   775
as clears the city from the guilt of death.
There, if she prays to Death, the only god

of her respect, she may manage not to die.
Or she may learn at last, though much too late,
how honoring the dead is wasted labor.   780

(*Exit Creon into the palace.*)°

CHORUS [*singing*]

STROPHE

Love unconquered in fight, love who falls on our possessions:°
You rest at night in the soft bloom of a girl's face.
You cross the sea, you are known in the wildest lairs.   785
Not the immortal gods can escape you,
nor men of a day. Who has you within him is mad.   790

ANTISTROPHE

You twist the minds of the just. Wrong they pursue and are ruined.
You made this quarrel of kindred men before us now.
Desire looks clear from the eyes of a lovely bride: 795
power as strong as the founded world.
Aphrodite, goddess, is playing, with whom no man can fight.   800

(*Antigone is brought from the palace under guard.*)

[*chanting*]
    Now I am carried beyond all bounds.
    My tears will not be checked.
    I see Antigone depart
    to the chamber where all must sleep.   805

ANTIGONE [*singing*]

STROPHE A

Men of my fathers' land, you see me go
my last journey. My last sight of the sun,
then never again. Death who brings all to sleep   810
takes me alive to the shore
of the river underground.
Not for me was the marriage hymn, nor will anyone start the song   815
at a wedding of mine. Acheron is my bridegroom.

CHORUS [*chanting*]

    With praise as your portion you go
    in fame to the vault of the dead.
    Untouched by wasting disease,
    not paying the price of the sword,   820
    of your own free will you go.
    Alone among mortals will you descend
    in life to the house of Death.

ANTIGONE [*singing*]

           ANTISTROPHE A

Pitiful was the death that Phrygian stranger died,
our queen once, Tantalus' daughter. The rock by Sipylus   825
covered her over, like stubborn ivy it grew.
Still, as she wastes, the rain
and snow companion her, so men say.
Pouring down from her mourning eyes comes the water that
soaks the stone.   830
My own putting to sleep a god has arranged like hers.

CHORUS [*chanting*]

    God's child and god she was:
    but we are born to death.   835
    Yet even in death you will have your fame,
    to have gone like a god to your fate,
    in living and dying alike.

ANTIGONE [*singing*]

           STROPHE B

Laughter against me now. In the name of our fathers' gods,
could you not wait till I went? Must affront be thrown in my face?   840
O city of wealthy men.
I call upon Dirce's spring,
I call upon Thebe's grove in the armored plain,   845
to be my witnesses, how with no friend's mourning,
by what decree I go to the fresh-made prison tomb.
Alive to the place of corpses, an alien still,   850
never at home with the living nor with the dead.

CHORUS

    You went to the furthest verge
    of daring, but there you tripped
    on the high pedestal of justice, and fell.   855
    Perhaps you are paying your father's pain.

ANTIGONE

          ANTISTROPHE B

You speak of my darkest thought, my pitiful father's fame,
spread through all the world, and the doom that haunts our house,   860
the glorious house of Labdacus.
My mother's marriage bed.
Destruction where she lay with her husband-son,   865
my father. These are my parents and I their child.
I go to stay with them. My curse is to die unwed.
My brother, you found your fate when you found your bride,   870
you found it for me as well. Dead, you destroy my life.

CHORUS

    You showed respect for the dead.
    So we for you: but power
    is not to be thwarted so.
    Your self-willed temper has brought you down.   875

ANTIGONE

          EPODE

Unwept, no wedding-song, unfriended, now I go
down the road made ready for me.
No longer am I allowed to see this holy light of the sun.   880
No friend bewails my fate.

                  (Creon enters from the palace.)°

CREON

When people sing the dirge for their own deaths
ahead of time, no one would ever stop
if they might hope that this would be of use.°
Take her away at once, and open up   885
the tomb I spoke of. Leave her there alone.

There let her choose: death, or a buried life.
No stain of guilt upon us in this case,
but she is exiled from our life on earth. 890

ANTIGONE
O tomb, O marriage chamber, hollowed-out
house that will watch forever, where I go—
to my own people, most of whom are there;
Persephone has taken them to her.
Last of them all, beyond the rest ill-fated, 895
I shall descend, before my course is run.
Still when I get there I may hope to find
I've come as a dear friend to my dear father,
to you, my mother, and my brother too.
All three of you have known my hand in death. 900
I washed your bodies, dressed them for the grave,
poured out the last libation at the tomb.
And now, Polyneices, you know the price I pay
for doing final service to your corpse.
       And yet the wise will know my choice was right.
Were I a mother, with children or husband dead, 905
I'd let them molder. I should not have chosen
in such a case to cross the state's decree.
What is the law that lies behind these words?
One husband gone, I might have found another,
or a child from a new man in the first child's place; 910
but with my parents covered up in death,
no brother for me, ever, could be born.
Such was the law by which I honored you.
But Creon thought the doing was a crime, 915
a dreadful daring, brother of my heart.
So now he takes and leads me out by force.
No marriage bed, no marriage song for me,
and since no wedding, so no child to rear.
I go, without a friend, struck down by fate,
living, to the hollow chambers of the dead. 920

What divine justice have I disobeyed?
Why, in my misery, look to the gods for help?
Can I call any of them my ally?
I stand convicted of impiety,
the evidence my pious duty done.
If the gods think that this is righteousness,   925
in suffering I'll see my error clear.
But if it is the others who are wrong
I wish them no greater punishment than mine.

CHORUS [*Chorus, Creon, and Antigone chanting in turn*]
The same tempest of mind
as ever, controls the girl.   930

CREON
Therefore her guards shall regret
the slowness with which they move.

ANTIGONE
That word comes close to death.

CREON
You are perfectly right in that;
I offer no grounds for hope.   935

ANTIGONE
O town of my fathers in Thebe's land,
O gods of our house!
I am led away and must not wait.
Look, leaders of Thebes,   940
I am last of your royal line.
Look what I suffer, at whose command,
because I respected the right.

(*Antigone is led away, to the side.*)

CHORUS [*singing*]
STROPHE A
Danaë suffered too.
She went from the light to the brass-built room,   945

[55] ANTIGONE

bedchamber and tomb together. Like you, poor child,
she was of great descent, and more, she held and kept
the seed of the golden rain which was Zeus.   950
Fate has terrible power.
You cannot escape it by wealth or war.
No fort will keep it out, no ships outrun it.

Remember the angry king,   955
son of Dryas, who raged against Dionysus and paid,
pent in a rock-walled prison. His bursting wrath
slowly went down. As the terror of madness went,
he learned of his frenzied attack on the god.   960
Fool, he had tried to stop
the dancing women possessed of god,
the fire of Bacchic rites, the songs and pipes.   965

STROPHE B

Where the dark rocks divide
sea from sea at the Bosporus,
is Thracian Salmydessus, where savage Ares   970
beheld the terrible blinding wounds
dealt to Phineus' sons by their father's wife.   975
Dark the eyes that looked to avenge their mother.
Sharp with her shuttle she struck, and blooded her hands.°

ANTISTROPHE B

Wasting they wept their fate,
settled when they were born   980
to Cleopatra, unhappy queen.
She was a princess too, of the ancient Erechthids,
but was reared in the cave of the wild North Wind, her father,   985
swift as a horse over the hills.
Half a goddess, still, child, she suffered like you.

(Enter, from the side, Teiresias, led by a boy attendant.)

TEIRESIAS

Elders of Thebes, we two have come one road,
two of us looking through one pair of eyes.
This is the way of walking for the blind. 990

CREON

Old Teiresias, what news has brought you here?

TEIRESIAS

I'll tell you. You in turn must trust the prophet.

CREON

I've always been attentive to your counsel.

TEIRESIAS

And therefore you have steered this city straight.

CREON

So I can say how helpful you have been. 995

TEIRESIAS

Again you are balanced on a razor's edge.

CREON

What is it? How I shudder at your words!

TEIRESIAS

You'll know, when you hear the signs that I have marked.
I sat where every bird of heaven comes 1000
in my old place of augury, and heard
bird cries I'd never known. They screeched about
goaded by madness, inarticulate.
I marked that they were tearing one another
with claws of murder. I could hear the wing-beats.
I was afraid, so straightaway I tried 1005
burnt sacrifice upon the flaming altar.
No fire caught my offerings. Slimy ooze
dripped on the ashes, smoked and sputtered there.
Gall burst its bladder, vanished into vapor; 1010

the fat dripped from the bones and would not burn.
These are the omens of the rites that failed,
as this boy here has told me. He's my guide
as I am guide to others.
Why has this sickness struck against the state?   1015
Through your decision.
All of the altars of the town are choked
with leavings of the dogs and birds; their feast
was on that fated, fallen son of Oedipus.
So the gods accept no offering from us,
not prayer, nor flame of sacrifice. The birds   1020
cry out a sound that I cannot distinguish,
gorged with the greasy blood of that dead man.

      Think of these things, my son. All men may err,
but error once committed, he's no fool
nor unsuccessful, who can change his mind   1025
and cure the trouble he has fallen in.
Stubbornness and stupidity are twins.
Yield to the dead. Why goad him where he lies?
What use to kill the dead a second time?   1030
I speak for your own good. And I am right.
Learning from a wise counselor is not pain
if what he speaks are profitable words.

CREON

    Old man, you all, like bowmen at a mark,
have bent your bows at me. I've had my share
of seers: I've been an item in your accounts.   1035
Make profit, trade in Lydian electrum,
pure gold of India; that's your chief desire.
But you will never cover up that corpse,
not if the very eagles tear their food   1040
from him, and leave it at the throne of Zeus.
I wouldn't give him up for burial
in fear of that pollution. For I know

no mortal being can pollute the gods.
Yes, old Teiresias, human beings fall;   1045
the clever ones the furthest, when they plead
a shameful case so well in hope of profit.

TEIRESIAS

Alas!
What man can tell me, has he thought at all . . .

CREON

What tired cliché's coming from your lips?

TEIRESIAS

How the best of all possessions is good counsel.   1050

CREON

And so is foolishness the worst of all.

TEIRESIAS

But you're infected with that same disease.

CREON

I'm reluctant to be uncivil to a seer . . .

TEIRESIAS

You're that already. You have said I lie.

CREON

Well, the whole crew of seers are money-mad.   1055

TEIRESIAS

And the whole tribe of tyrants grab at gain.

CREON

Do you realize you are talking to a king?

TEIRESIAS

I know. Who helped you save this town you hold?

CREON

You're a wise seer, but you love wickedness.

TEIRESIAS

You'll bring me to speak the unspeakable, very soon.   1060

CREON

Well, speak it out. But do not speak for profit.

TEIRESIAS

Do I seem to have spoken for profit, with regard to you?

CREON

Know this, that you can't buy and sell my policies.

TEIRESIAS

Know well yourself, the sun won't roll its course   1065
many more days, before you come to give
corpse for these corpses, child of your own loins.
For you've confused the upper and lower worlds.
You settled a living person without honor
in a tomb; you keep up here that which belongs   1070
below, a corpse unburied and unholy.
Not you, nor any god on high should have
any business with this. The violation's yours.
So the patient, foul punishers lie in wait
to track you down: the Furies sent by Hades   1075
and by all gods will even you with your victims.
Now say that I am bribed! The time is close
when men and women shall wail within your house,
and all the cities that you fought in war°   1080
whose sons had burial from wild beasts, or dogs,
or birds that brought the stench of your great wrong
back to each hearth, they all will move against you.
A bowman, as you said, I send my shafts,   1085
since you provoked me, straight. You'll feel the wound.
      Boy, take me home now. Let him spend his rage
on younger men, and learn to calm his tongue,
and keep a better mind than now he does.   1090

                                        (Exit, to the side.)

CHORUS LEADER

Lord, he has gone. Terrible prophecies!
And since the time my hair turned gray from black,
his sayings to the city have been true.

CREON

I also know this. And my mind is torn.   1095
To yield is dreadful. But to stand against him,
and shatter my spirit in doom is dreadful too.

CHORUS LEADER

Now you must seek good counsel, and take advice.

CREON

What must I do? Speak, and I shall obey.

CHORUS LEADER

Go free the maiden from that rocky house;   1100
and bury the dead who lies in readiness.

CREON

This is your counsel? You would have me yield?

CHORUS LEADER

Quick as you can. The gods move very fast
when they bring ruin on misguided men.

CREON

How hard, abandonment of my desire!   1105
But I can fight necessity no more.

CHORUS LEADER

Do it yourself. Leave it to no one else.

CREON

I'll go at once. Come, followers, to your work.
You that are here round up the other fellows.
Take axes with you, hurry to that place
that overlooks us there.   1110
And I, since my decision's overturned,

the one who bound her will set her free myself.
I've come to fear it's best to hold the laws
of old tradition to the end of life.

(Exit, to the side.)

CHORUS [*singing*]

STROPHE A

God of the many names, Semele's proud delight,   1115
child of Olympian thunder, Italy's master,
lord of Eleusis, where all men come   1120
to Mother Demeter's plain:
Bacchus, who dwell in Thebes,
by Ismenus' running water,
where wild Bacchic women are at home,
on the soil of the dragon seed.   1125

ANTISTROPHE A

Seen in the glaring flame, high on the double crags,
with the nymphs of Parnassus at play on the hill,
seen by Castalia's fresh fountain: 1130
you come from the ivied heights
and the green grape-filled coast of Euboea.
In immortal words they cry
your name, lord, who watch the roads,   1135
the many streets of Thebes.

STROPHE B

This is your city, honored beyond the rest,
the town of your mother's miracle-death.
Now, as we wrestle with grim disease,   1140
come with healing step along Parnassus' slope
or over the resounding sea.   1145

ANTISTROPHE B

Leader in dance of the fire-pulsing stars,
overseer of the voices of night,
child of Zeus, be manifest,

with due companionship of maenads dancing   1150
and honoring their lord, Iacchus.

(Enter Messenger, from the side.)

MESSENGER

Neighbors of Cadmus, and Amphion's house,   1155
there is no kind of state in human life
which I would now dare either praise or blame.
Fortune sets straight, and Fortune overturns
the happy or unhappy, day by day.
No prophecy can deal with men's affairs.   1160
Creon was envied once, as I believe,
for having saved this city from its foes
and having got full power in this land.
He steered it well. And he had noble sons.
Now everything is gone.   1165
Yes, when a man has lost all happiness,
he's not alive. Call him a breathing corpse.
Be very rich at home. Live as a king.
But once your joy has gone, though these are left
they are smoke's shadow to lost happiness.   1170

CHORUS LEADER
What is the grief of princes that you bring?

MESSENGER
They're dead. The living are responsible.

CHORUS LEADER
Who died? Who did the murder? Tell us now.

MESSENGER
Haemon is gone. His own flesh and blood did him in.   1175

CHORUS LEADER
But whose arm struck? His father's or his own?

MESSENGER
He killed himself, angry at his father's killing.

CHORUS LEADER

Seer, all too true the prophecy you told!

MESSENGER

This is the state of things. Now make your plans.

(Enter Eurydice, from the palace.)

CHORUS LEADER

Eurydice is with us now, I see.   1180
Creon's poor wife. She may have come by chance.
She may have heard something about her son.

EURYDICE

I heard your talk as I was coming out
to greet the goddess Pallas with my prayer.   `   1185
And as I moved the bolts that held the door
I heard the voice of family disaster.
I fell back fainting in my women's arms.
But say again, just what is the news you bring.   1190
I, whom you speak to, have known grief before.

MESSENGER

Dear lady, I was there, and I shall tell,
leaving out nothing of the true account.
Why should I make it soft for you with tales
to prove myself a liar? Truth is right.   1195
I followed your husband to the plain's far edge,
where Polyneices' corpse was lying still
unpitied. The dogs had torn him all apart.
We prayed the goddess of all journeyings,
and Pluto, that they turn their wrath to kindness;   1200
we gave the final purifying bath,
then burned the poor remains on new-cut boughs,
and heaped a high mound of his native earth.
Then turned we to the maiden's rocky bed,
approaching Hades' hollow marriage chamber.   1205
But, still far off, one of us heard a voice
in keen lament by that unblest abode.

He ran and told the master. As Creon came
he heard confusion crying. He groaned and spoke: 1210
"Am I a prophet now, and do I tread
the saddest of all roads I ever trod?
My son's voice crying! Servants, run up close,
stand by the tomb and look, push through the crevice   1215
where we built the pile of rock, right to the entry.
Find out if that is Haemon's voice I hear
or if the gods are tricking me indeed."
We obeyed the order of our mournful master.
In the far corner of the tomb we saw   1220
her, hanging by the neck, caught in a noose
of her own linen veiling.
Haemon embraced her as she hung, and mourned
his bride's destruction, dead and gone below,
his father's actions, the unfated marriage.   1225
When Creon saw him, he groaned terribly,
and went toward him, and called him with lament:
"What have you done, what did you have in mind,
what happened so as thus to ruin you?
Come out, my child, I do beseech you, come!"   1230
The boy looked at him with his angry eyes,
spat in his face and spoke no further word.
He drew his sword, but as his father ran,
he missed his aim. Then the unhappy boy,
in anger at himself, leant on the blade: 1235
it entered, half its length, into his side.
While he was conscious he embraced the maiden,
holding her gently. Last, he gasped out blood,
red blood on her white cheek.
Corpse on a corpse he lies. He found his marriage,   1240
its celebration in the halls of Hades.
So he has made it very clear to men
that to reject good counsel is a crime.

(Exit Eurydice, back into the palace.)

CHORUS LEADER

What do you make of this? The queen has gone
in silence, with no word of evil or of good.   1245

MESSENGER

I wonder at her, too. But we can hope
that she has gone to mourn her son within
with her own women, not before the town.
She knows discretion. She will do no wrong.   1250

CHORUS LEADER

I am not sure. This muteness may portend
as great disaster as a loud lament.

MESSENGER

I will go in and see if some deep plan
hides in her heart's wild pain. You may be right.   1255
There can be heavy danger in mute grief.

(*Exit the Messenger into the palace. Creon enters from the side
with his followers. They are carrying Haemon's body on a bier.*)

CHORUS [*chanting*]

But look, the king draws near.
His own hand brings
the witness of his crime,
the doom he brought on himself.   1260

CREON [*singing in what follows, while the Chorus and Messenger speak*]

STROPHE A

O crimes of my wicked heart,
harshness bringing death.
You see the killer, you see the kin he killed.
My planning was all unblest.   1265
Son, you have died too soon.
Oh, you have gone away
through my fault, not your own.

CHORUS LEADER

You have learned justice, though it comes too late.   1270

CREON

Yes, I have learned in sorrow. It was a god who struck,
who has weighted my head with disaster; he drove me to wild
*   strange ways,*
his heavy heel on my joy.   1275
Oh sorrows, sorrows of men.

(Reenter the Messenger, from the palace.)

MESSENGER

Master, you hold one sorrow in your hands
but you have more, stored up inside the house.   1280

CREON

What further suffering can come on me?

MESSENGER

Your wife has died. The dead man's mother indeed,
poor soul, with wounds freshly inflicted.

CREON

ANTISTROPHE A

Hades, harbor of all,
you have destroyed me now.   1285
Terrible news to hear, horror the tale you tell.
I was dead, and you kill me again.
Boy, did I hear you right?   1290
Did you say the queen was dead,
slaughter on slaughter heaped?

(The central doors of the palace open, and
the corpse of Eurydice is revealed.)

CHORUS LEADER

Now you can see. Concealment is all over.

CREON

My second sorrow is here. Surely no fate remains   1295
which can strike me again. Just now, I held my son in my arms.
And now I see her dead.
Woe for the mother and son.   1300

MESSENGER

There, by the altar, dying on the sword,°
her eyes fell shut. She wept her older son,
Megareus, who died before, and this one. Finally
she cursed you as the killer of her children.   1305

CREON

STROPHE B

I am mad with fear. Will no one strike
and kill me with cutting sword?
Sorrowful, soaked in sorrow to the bone!   1310

MESSENGER

Yes, for she held you guilty in the death
of him before you, and the elder dead.

CREON

How did she die?

MESSENGER

Struck home at her own heart   1315
when she had heard of Haemon's suffering.

CREON

This is my guilt, all mine. I killed you, I say it clear.
Servants, take me away, out of the sight of men.   1320
I who am nothing more than nothing now.   1325

CHORUS LEADER

Your plan is good—if any good is left.
Best to cut short our sorrow.

CREON

ANTISTROPHE B

Let me go, let me go. May death come quick,
bringing my final day!   1330
O let me never see tomorrow's dawn.

CHORUS LEADER

That is the future's. We must look to now.
What will be is in other hands than ours.   1335

CREON

All my desire was in that prayer of mine.

CHORUS LEADER

Pray not again. No mortal can escape
the doom prepared for him.

CREON [*singing*]

Take me away at once, the frantic man who killed   1340
my son, against my meaning, and you too, my wife.
I cannot look at either, I cannot rest.
My life is warped past cure. Fate unbearable   1345
has leapt down on my head.

(Creon and his attendants enter the palace.)

CHORUS [*chanting*]

Our happiness depends
on wisdom all the way.
The gods must have their due.
Great words by men of pride   1350
bring greater blows upon them.
So wisdom comes to the old.

OEDIPUS THE KING

Translated by DAVID GRENE

OEDIPUS THE KING

Characters   OEDIPUS, king of Thebes
A PRIEST
CREON, his brother-in-law (Jocasta's brother)
CHORUS of old men of Thebes
TEIRESIAS, an old blind prophet
JOCASTA, his wife (and mother)
FIRST MESSENGER
A HERDSMAN
SECOND MESSENGER

Scene: In front of the palace of Oedipus at Thebes. On one side stands the Priest with a crowd of children.

(Enter Oedipus, from the palace door.)

OEDIPUS
    Children, young sons and daughters of old Cadmus,
why do you sit here with your suppliant crowns?
The town is heavy with a mingled burden
of sounds and smells, of groans and hymns and incense;   5
I did not think it fit that I should hear
of this from messengers but came myself—
I, Oedipus whom all men call the Great.

(To the Priest.)

    You're old and they are young; come, speak for them.
What do you fear or want, that you sit here   10
suppliant? Indeed I'm willing to give all

that you may need; I would be very hard
should I not pity suppliants like these.

PRIEST
O ruler of my country, Oedipus,
you see our company around the altar;   15
you see our ages; some of us, like these,
who cannot yet fly far, and some of us
heavy with age; these children are the chosen
among the young, and I the priest of Zeus.
Within the market place sit others crowned   20
with suppliant garlands, at the double shrine
of Pallas and the temple where Ismenus
gives oracles by fire. King, you yourself
have seen our city reeling like a wreck
already; it can scarcely lift its prow
out of the depths, out of the bloody surf.
A blight is on the fruitful plants of the earth,   25
a blight is on the cattle in the fields,
a blight is on our women that no children
are born to them; a god that carries fire,
a deadly pestilence, is on our town,
strikes us and spares not, and the house of Cadmus
is emptied of its people while black Death
grows rich in groaning and in lamentation.   30
        We have not come as suppliants to this altar
because we think of you as of a god,
but rather judging you the first of men
in all the chances of this life and when
we mortals have to do with more than man.
You came and by your coming saved our city,   35
freed us from tribute which we paid of old
to the Sphinx, cruel singer. This you did
in virtue of no knowledge we could give you,
in virtue of no teaching; it was god
that aided you, men say, and you are held

with god's assistance to have saved our lives.
        Now Oedipus, greatest in all men's eyes,   40
here falling at your feet we all entreat you,
find us some strength for rescue.
Perhaps you'll hear a wise word from some god,
perhaps you will learn something from a man
(for I have seen that for those with experience
the outcomes of their counsels live the most).   45
Noblest of men, go, and raise up our city,
go—and give heed. For now this land of ours
calls you its savior since you saved it once.
So, let us never speak about your reign
as of a time when first our feet were set   50
secure and straight, but later fell to ruin.
Raise up our city, save it and set it straight.
Once you have brought us luck with happy omen;
be no less now in fortune.
If you will rule this land, as now you rule it,
better to rule it full of men than empty.   55
For neither tower nor ship is anything
when empty, and none live in it together.

OEDIPUS

I pity you, children. You have come full of longing,
but I have known the story before you told it
only too well. I know you are all sick,   60
yet there is not one of you, sick though you are,
that is as sick as I myself.
Your several sorrows each have single scope
and touch but one of you. My spirit groans
for city and myself and you at once.
You have not roused me like a man from sleep;   65
know that I have given many tears to this,
gone many ways wandering in thought.
But as I thought I found only one remedy
and that I took. I sent Menoeceus' son

Creon, Jocasta's brother, to Apollo,
to his Pythian temple,   70
that he might learn there by what act or word
I could save this city. As I count the days,
it worries me what he's doing; he is gone
far longer than he needed for the journey.   75
But when he comes, then, may I prove a villain,
if I shall not do all the god commands.

PRIEST

Your words are opportune: for here, your men
signal that Creon is this moment coming.

OEDIPUS

O holy lord Apollo, may his news   80
be bright for us and bring us light and safety.°

PRIEST

It is happy news, I think, for else his head
would not be crowned with sprigs of fruitful laurel.

                              (Enter Creon, from one side.)

OEDIPUS

We will know soon,
he's within hail. Lord Creon, my good kinsman,   85
what is the word you bring us from the god?

CREON

A good word—for even things quite hard to bear,
if the final issue turns out well,
I count complete good fortune.

OEDIPUS

What do you mean? What you have said so far
leaves me uncertain whether to trust or fear.   90

CREON

If you'll hear my news in the presence of these others
I am ready to speak, or else to go within.

OEDIPUS

  Speak it to all; the grief I bear, I bear it
  more for these people than for my own life.

CREON

  I will tell you, then, what I heard from the god.   95
  King Phoebus in plain words commanded us
  to drive out a pollution from our land,
  pollution grown ingrained within the soil;
  drive it out, said the god, not cherish it,
  till it's past cure.

OEDIPUS

                    What is the rite
  of purification? How shall it be done?

CREON

  By banishing a man, or expiation   100
  of blood by blood, since it is murder guilt
  which shakes our city in this destroying storm.

OEDIPUS

  Who is this man whose fate the god pronounces?

CREON

  My Lord, before you piloted the state
  we had a king called Laius.

OEDIPUS

  I know of him by hearsay. I never saw him.   105

CREON

  The god commanded clearly: that we must
  punish with force this dead man's murderers,
  whoever they are.

OEDIPUS

  Where are they in the world? Where would a trace
  of this old crime be found? It would be hard
  to guess where.

CREON

    The guilt is in this land;   110
    that which is sought can be found;
    the unheeded thing escapes:
    so said the god.

OEDIPUS

    Was it at home, or in the countryside
    that death came to Laius, or traveling abroad?

CREON

    He left, he said himself, upon an embassy,
    but never returned after he set out from home.   115

OEDIPUS

    Was there no messenger, no fellow traveler
    who saw what happened? Such a one might tell
    something of use.

CREON

    They were all killed save one. He fled in terror
    and he could tell us nothing in clear terms
    of what he knew, except for one thing only.

OEDIPUS

    What was it?
    If we could even find a slim beginning   120
    in which to hope, we might discover much.

CREON

    This man said that the robbers they encountered
    were many and the hands that did the murder
    were many; it was no man's single power.

OEDIPUS

    How could a robber dare a deed like this
    were he not helped with money from the city?   125

CREON

    That indeed was thought. But Laius was dead
    and in our trouble there was none to help.

OEDIPUS

What trouble was so great to hinder you
inquiring out the murder of your king?

CREON

The riddling Sphinx induced us to neglect   130
mysterious crimes and rather seek solution
of troubles at our feet.

OEDIPUS

I'll begin again and bring this all to light.
Fittingly King Phoebus took this care
about the dead, and you too, fittingly.
And justly you will see in me an ally,   135
a champion of this country and the god.
For when I drive pollution from the land
I will not serve a distant friend's advantage,
but act in my own interest. Whoever
he was that killed the king may readily
wish to dispatch me with his murderous hand;   140
so helping the dead king I help myself.
      Come, children, take your suppliant boughs and go;
up from the altars now. Call the assembly
and let the people of Cadmus meet and know
that I'll do everything. God will decide   145
whether we shall prosper or shall fail.

PRIEST

Rise, children—it was this we came to seek,
which of himself the king now offers us.
May Phoebus who gave us the oracle
come to our rescue and stop the plague.   150

(Exit all. The Chorus enters from the side.)

CHORUS [*singing*]

STROPHE A

What is the sweet spoken word of god from the shrine of Pytho
rich in gold

that has come to glorious Thebes?
I am stretched on the rack of doubt, and terror and trembling hold
my heart, O Delian Healer, and I worship full of fears   155
for what doom you will bring to pass, new or renewed in the
revolving years.
Speak to me, immortal voice,
child of golden Hope.

ANTISTROPHE A

First I call on you, Athena, deathless daughter of Zeus,
and Artemis, Earth upholder,   160
who sits in the midst of the marketplace in the throne which
men call Fame,
and Phoebus, the far-shooter, three averters of Fate,
come to us now, if ever before, when ruin rushed upon the state,   165
you drove destruction's flame away
out of our land.

STROPHE B

Our sorrows defy number;
all the ship's timbers are rotten;
taking of thought is no spear for the driving away of the plague.   170
There are no growing children in this famous land;
there are no women bearing the pangs of childbirth.
You may see them one with another, like birds swift on the wing,   175
quicker than fire unmastered,
speeding away to the coast of the Western god.

ANTISTROPHE B

In the unnumbered deaths
of its people the city dies;   180
the children that are born lie dead on the naked earth
unpitied, spreading contagion of death; and grey-haired mothers
and wives
everywhere stand at the altar's edge, suppliant, moaning;   185
the hymn to the healing god rings out, but with it the wailing
voices are blended.

From these our sufferings grant us, O golden Daughter of Zeus,
glad-faced deliverance.

There is no clash of brazen shields but our fight is with the war god,   190
a war god ringed with the cries of men, a savage god who burns us;
grant that he turn in racing course backward out of our country's
    bounds
to the great palace of Amphitrite or where the waves of the
    Thracian sea   195
deny the stranger safe anchorage.
Whatsoever escapes the night
at last the light of day revisits;°
so smite him, Father Zeus,
beneath your thunderbolt,   200
for you are the lord of the lightning, the lightning that carries fire.

And your unconquered arrow shafts, winged by the
    golden-corded bow,
Lycian king, I beg to be at our side for help;
and the gleaming torches of Artemis with which she scours the
Lycian hills,   205
and I call on the god with the turban of gold, who gave his name
to this country of ours,   210
the Bacchic god with the wind-flushed face,
you who travel with the maenad company crying Euhoi,
come with your torch of pine;
for the god that is our enemy is a god unhonored among the gods.   215

(Enter Oedipus.)

OEDIPUS
    For what you ask me—if you will hear my words,
    and hearing welcome them and fight the plague,
    you will find strength and lightening of your load.
    Listen now to me; what I say to you, I say
    as one that is a stranger to the story   220

as stranger to the deed. For I would not
be far upon the track if I alone
were tracing it without a clue or helper.
But since, though late, I also have become
a citizen among you, citizens—
now I proclaim to all the men of Thebes:
who so among you knows the murderer
by whose hand Laius, son of Labdacus,   225
died—I command him to tell everything
to me—yes, though he fears himself to take the blame
on his own head; for bitter punishment
he shall have none, but leave this land unharmed.
Or if he knows the murderer, another,   230
maybe a foreigner, still let him speak the truth.
For I will pay him and be grateful, too.
But if you shall keep silence, if perhaps
some one of you, to shield a guilty friend,
or for his own sake shall reject my words—
hear what I shall do then: 235
I forbid that man, whoever he be, my land,
this land where I hold sovereignty and throne;
and I forbid any to welcome him
or give him greeting or make him a sharer
in sacrifice or offering to the gods,
or give him water for his hands to wash.   240
I command all to drive him from their homes,
since he is our pollution, as the oracle
of Pytho's god proclaimed him now to me.
So I stand forth a champion of the god
and of the man who died.   245
Upon the murderer I invoke this curse—°
whether he is one man and all unknown,
or one of many—may he wear out his life
in misery to miserable doom!
If with my knowledge he lives at my hearth   250
I pray that I myself may feel my curse.

On you I lay my charge to fulfill all this
for me, for the god, and for this land of ours
destroyed and blighted, by the gods forsaken.
Even were this no matter of god's ordinance   255
it did not fit you so to leave it lie,
unpurified, since a great man is dead,
a king. Indeed, you should have searched it out.
Since I am now the holder of his office,
and have his bed and wife that once was his,   260
and had his line not been unfortunate
we would have children in common—(but fortune leaped
upon his head)—because of all these things,
I fight in his defense as for my father,   265
and I shall try all means to take the murderer
of Laius the son of Labdacus
the son of Polydorus and before him
of Cadmus and before him of Agenor.
    Those who do not obey me, may the gods
grant no crops springing from the ground they plough   270
nor children to their women! May a fate
like this, or one still worse than this, consume them!
For you whom these words please, the other Thebans,
may Justice as your ally and all the gods
live with you, blessing you now and for ever!   275

CHORUS LEADER
    As you have held me to my oath, I speak:
    I neither killed the king nor can declare
    the killer; but since Phoebus set the quest
    it is his part to tell us who has done it.

OEDIPUS
    Right; but to put compulsion on the gods   280
    against their will—no man can do that.

CHORUS LEADER
    May I then say what I think second best?

OEDIPUS
If there's a third best, too, spare not to tell it.

CHORUS LEADER
I know that what the lord Teiresias
sees is most often what the lord Apollo   285
sees. If you should inquire of this from him
you might find out most clearly.

OEDIPUS
Even in this my actions have not been slow.
On Creon's word I have sent two messengers,
and why the prophet is not here already
I have been wondering.

CHORUS LEADER
                                    His skill apart,
there is besides only an old faint story.   290

OEDIPUS
What is it? I look at every rumor.

CHORUS LEADER
It was said that he was killed by certain wayfarers.

OEDIPUS
I heard that, too, but no one sees who did it.°

CHORUS LEADER
Yet if he has a share of fear at all,
his courage will not stand firm, hearing your curse.   295

OEDIPUS
The man who in the doing did not shrink
will fear no word.

CHORUS LEADER
    Here comes his prosecutor:
led by these men the godly prophet comes,
in whom alone of humankind the truth
is his by nature.

OEDIPUS

Teiresias, you are versed in everything,   300
things teachable and things not to be spoken,
things of the heaven and earth-creeping things.
You have no eyes but in your mind you know
with what a plague our city is afflicted.
My lord, in you alone we find a champion,
in you alone one that can rescue us.
Perhaps you have not heard the messengers,   305
but Phoebus sent in answer to our sending
an oracle declaring that our freedom
from this disease would only come when we
should learn the names of those who killed King Laius,
and kill them or expel from our country.
Do not begrudge us messages from birds,   310
or any other way of prophecy
within your skill; save yourself and the city,
save me; save all of us from this pollution
that lies on us because of that dead man.
We are in your hands; it's a man's most noble labor
to help another when he has the means and power.   315

TEIRESIAS

Alas, how terrible is wisdom when
it brings no profit to the man that's wise!
This I knew well, but had forgotten it,
else I would not have come here.

OEDIPUS

                        What is this?
How gloomy you are now you've come!

TEIRESIAS

                                Let me
go home. It will be easiest for us both   320

to bear our several destinies to the end
if you will follow my advice.

OEDIPUS
                    You'd rob us
of this your gift of prophecy? You talk
as one who had no care for law nor love
for Thebes who reared you.

TEIRESIAS
    Yes, but I see that even your own words
    miss the mark; therefore I must fear for mine.   325

OEDIPUS
    For god's sake if you know of anything,
    do not turn from us; all of us kneel to you,
    all of us here, your suppliants.

TEIRESIAS
    All of you here know nothing. I will not
    bring to the light of day my troubles, mine—
    rather than call them yours.

OEDIPUS
        What do you mean?
    You know of something but refuse to speak.   330
    Would you betray us and destroy the city?

TEIRESIAS
    I will not bring this pain upon us both,
    neither on you nor on myself. Why is it
    you question me and waste your labor? I
    will tell you nothing.

OEDIPUS
    You would provoke a stone! Tell us, you villain,
    tell us, and do not stand there quietly   335
    unmoved, unhelpful, set on doing nothing.

TEIRESIAS

You blame my temper but you do not see
your own that lives within you; so you chide
me instead.

OEDIPUS

Who would not feel his temper rise
at words like these with which you shame our city?   340

TEIRESIAS

Of themselves things will come, although I hide them
and breathe no word of them.

OEDIPUS

                          Since they will come
tell them to me.

TEIRESIAS

                          I will say nothing further.
Against this answer let your temper rage
as wildly as you will.

OEDIPUS

                          Indeed I am
so angry I shall not hold back a jot   345
of what I think. For I would have you know
I think you were coplotter of the deed
and doer of the deed save insofar
as for the actual killing. Had you had eyes
I would have said alone you murdered him.

TEIRESIAS

Yes? Then I warn you faithfully to keep   350
the letter of your proclamation and
from this day forth to speak no word of greeting
to these nor me; you are the land's pollution.

OEDIPUS

How shamelessly you started up this taunt!
How do you think you will escape?   355

TEIRESIAS
          I have.
I have escaped; the truth is what I cherish
and that's my strength.

OEDIPUS
          And who has taught you truth?
Not your profession surely!

TEIRESIAS
          You have taught me,
for you have made me speak against my will.

OEDIPUS
Speak what? Tell me again that I may learn it better.

TEIRESIAS
Did you not understand before or would you   360
provoke me into speaking?

OEDIPUS
          I did not grasp it,
not so to call it known. Say it again.

TEIRESIAS
I say you are the murderer of the king
whose murderer you seek.

OEDIPUS
          Not twice you shall
say ghastly things like this and stay unpunished.

TEIRESIAS
Shall I say more to tempt your anger further?

OEDIPUS
As much as you wish; it will be said in vain.   365

TEIRESIAS
I say that, unknowing, with those you love the best

you live in foulest shame unconsciously
and do not see where you are in calamity.

OEDIPUS

Do you imagine you can always talk
like this, and live to rejoice at it hereafter?

TEIRESIAS

Yes, if the truth has anything of strength.

OEDIPUS

It has, but not for you; it has no strength   370
for you because you are blind in mind and ears
as well as in your eyes.

TEIRESIAS

                  You are a poor wretch
to taunt me with the very insults which
everyone soon will heap upon yourself.

OEDIPUS

Your life is one long night so that you cannot
hurt me or any other who sees the light.   375

TEIRESIAS

It is not fate that I should be your ruin,
Apollo is enough; it is his care
to work this out.

OEDIPUS

                  Was this your own design
or Creon's?

TEIRESIAS

                  Creon is no hurt to you.
but you are to yourself.

OEDIPUS

Wealth, kingly rule, and skill outmatching skill   380

for the contrivance of an envied life!
How great a store of jealousy you are hoarding,
if, for the sake of the office which I hold,
given me by the city, not sought by me,
my friend Creon, friend from the first and loyal,   385
thus secretly attacks me, secretly
desires to drive me out and secretly
suborns this juggling, trick-devising quack,
this wily beggar who has only eyes
for his own gains, but blindness in his skill.

    For, tell me, where have you seen clear, Teiresias,   390
with your prophetic mind? When the dark singer,
the Sphinx, was in your country, did you speak
word of deliverance to these citizens?
Yet solving the riddle then was not the province
of a chance comer: it was a prophet's task,
and plainly you had no such gift of prophecy
from birds nor otherwise from any god   395
to glean a word of knowledge. But I came,
Oedipus, who knew nothing, and I stopped her.
I solved the riddle by my wit alone.
Mine was no knowledge got from birds. And now
you would expel me,
because you think that you will find a place   400
by Creon's throne. I think you will be sorry,
both you and your accomplice, for your plot
to drive me out. And did I not regard you
as an old man, some suffering would have taught you
that what was in your heart was treason.

CHORUS LEADER
We look at this man's words and yours, my king,
and we find both have spoken them in anger.   405
We need no angry words but only thought
how we may best hit the god's meaning for us.

TEIRESIAS

    If you are king, at least I have the right
    no less to speak in my defense against you.
    Of that much I am master. I am no slave
    of yours, but Loxias', and so I shall not   410
    enroll myself with Creon for my patron.
    Since you have taunted me with being blind,
    here is my word for you.
    You have your eyes but see not where you are
    in evil, nor where you live, nor whom you live with.
    Do you know who your parents are? Unknowing   415
    you are an enemy to kith and kin
    in death, beneath the earth, and in this life.
    A deadly footed, double-striking curse,
    from father and mother both, shall drive you forth
    out of this land, with darkness on your eyes,
    that now have such straight vision. Shall there be
    a place will not be harbor to your cries,   420
    a corner of Cithaeron will not ring°
    in echo to your laments, soon, soon,
    when you shall learn the secret of your marriage,
    which steered you to a haven in this house,
    haven no haven, after lucky voyage?
    And of the multitude of other evils
    establishing a grim equality°   425
    between you and your children, you know nothing.
    So, muddy with contempt my words and Creon's!
    Misery shall grind no man as it will you.

OEDIPUS

    Is it endurable that I should hear
    such words from him? Go and a curse go with you!   430
    Quick, home with you! Away from my house at once!

TEIRESIAS

    I would not have come either, had you not called me.

OEDIPUS

I did not know then you would talk like a fool—
or it would have been long before I called you.

TEIRESIAS

I am a fool then, as it seems to you—   435
but to the parents who begot you, wise.

OEDIPUS

What parents? Stop! Who are they of all the world?

TEIRESIAS

This day will show your birth and will destroy you.

OEDIPUS

How needlessly your riddles darken everything.

TEIRESIAS

But aren't you best at answering such riddles?   440

OEDIPUS

Yes. Taunt me where you will find me great.

TEIRESIAS

It is this very luck that has destroyed you.

OEDIPUS

I do not care, if it has saved this city.

TEIRESIAS

Well, I will go. Come, boy, lead me away.

OEDIPUS

Yes, lead him off. So long as you are here,   445
you are a stumbling block and a vexation;
once gone, you will not trouble me again.

TEIRESIAS

I have said
what I came here to say not fearing your
countenance: there is no way you can hurt me.

I tell you, king, this man, this murderer   450
(whom you have long declared you are in search of,
indicting him in threatening proclamation
as murderer of Laius)—he is here.
In name he is a stranger among citizens
but soon he will be shown to be homegrown,
true native Theban, and he'll have no joy
of the discovery: blindness for sight
and beggary for riches his exchange,   455
he shall go journeying to a foreign country
tapping his way before him with a stick.
He shall be proved father and brother both
to his own children in his house; to her
that gave him birth, a son and husband both;
a fellow sower in his father's bed
with that same father that he murdered.   460
Go within, reckon that out, and if you find me
mistaken, say I have no skill in prophecy.

(Exit separately, Teiresias to the side, Oedipus indoors.)

CHORUS [*singing*]

STROPHE A

Who is the man proclaimed
by Delphi's prophetic rock
as the bloody-handed murderer,   465
the doer of deeds that none dare name?
Now is the time for him to run
with a stronger foot
than wind-swift Pegasus
for the child of Zeus leaps in arms upon him   470
with fire and the lightning bolt,
and terribly close on his heels
are the Fates that never miss.

ANTISTROPHE A

Lately from snowy Parnassus
clearly the voice flashed forth,

bidding everyone track him down,   475
the unknown murderer.
In the savage forests he lurks and in
the caverns like
the mountain bull.
He is sad and lonely, and lonely his feet°
that carry him far from the navel of earth;   480
but its prophecies, ever living,
flutter around his head.

The skilled bird-prophet bewilders me terribly;
I do not approve what was said
nor can I deny it.   485
I do not know what to say;
I am in a flutter of foreboding;
I do not see the present
nor the past; I never heard of a quarrel between
the sons of Labdacus and of Polybus,
neither in the past nor now,   490
that I might bring as proof
in attacking the popular fame
of Oedipus, seeking   495
to take vengeance for undiscovered
death in the line of Labdacus.

Truly Zeus and Apollo are wise
and in human things all-knowing;
but amongst men there is no
distinct judgment, between the prophet
and me—which of us is right.   500
One man may pass another in wisdom
but I would never agree
with those that find fault with the king
till I should see the word   505
proved right beyond doubt. For once

in visible form the Sphinx
came against him, and all of us
saw his wisdom and in that test   510
he saved the city. So he will not be condemned by my mind.

(Enter Creon, from the side.)

CREON
Citizens, I have come because I heard
deadly words spread about me, that the king
accuses me. I cannot take that from him.   515
If he believes that in these present troubles
he has been wronged by me in word or deed
I do not want to live on with the burden
of such a scandal on me. The report
injures me doubly and most vitally—   520
for I'll be called a traitor to my city
and traitor also to my friends and you.

CHORUS LEADER
Perhaps it was a sudden gust of anger
that forced that insult from him, and no judgment.

CREON
But did he say that it was in compliance   525
with schemes of mine that the seer told him lies?

CHORUS LEADER
Yes, he said that, but why, I do not know.

CREON
Were his eyes straight in his head? Was his mind right
when he accused me in this fashion?

CHORUS LEADER
I do not know; I have no eyes to see   530
what princes do. Here comes the king himself.

(Enter Oedipus, from the palace.)

OEDIPUS

You, sir, how is it you come here? Have you so much
brazen-faced daring that you venture to
my house although you are proved manifestly
the murderer of that man, and though you tried,
openly, highway robbery of my crown?   535
For god's sake, tell me what you saw in me,
what cowardice or what stupidity,
that made you lay a plot like this against me?
Did you imagine I should not observe
your crafty scheme that stole upon me or
seeing it, take no means to counter it?
Was it not stupid of you to make the attempt,   540
to try to hunt down royal power without
the people at your back or friends? For only
with the people at your back and money can
this hunt end in the capture of a crown.

CREON

Do you know what you're doing? Will you listen
to words to answer yours, and then pass judgment?

OEDIPUS

You're quick to speak, but I am slow to grasp you,   545
for I have found you dangerous—and my foe.

CREON

First of all hear what I shall say to that.

OEDIPUS

At least don't tell me that you are not guilty.

CREON

If you think obstinacy without wisdom
a valuable possession, you are wrong.   550

OEDIPUS

And you are wrong if you believe that one
can harm a kinsman and then not be punished.

CREON
    This is but just—
    but tell me, then, of what offense I'm guilty.

OEDIPUS
    Did you or did you not urge me to send   555
    to this prophetic mumbler?

CREON
    I did indeed,
    and I shall stand by what I told you.

OEDIPUS
    How long ago is it since Laius . . .

CREON
    What about Laius? I don't understand.

OEDIPUS
    Vanished—died—was murdered?   560

CREON
                        It is long,
    a long, long time to reckon.

OEDIPUS
                        Was this prophet
    in the profession then?

CREON
                        He was, and honored
    as highly as he is today.

OEDIPUS
    At that time did he say a word about me?

CREON
    Never, at least when I was near him.   565

OEDIPUS
    You never made a search for the killer?°

CREON

We searched, indeed, but never learned of anything.

OEDIPUS

Why did our wise old friend not say this then?

CREON

I don't know; and when I know nothing, I
usually hold my tongue.

OEDIPUS

You know this much,   570
and can declare it if you are truly loyal.

CREON

What is it? If I know, I'll not deny it.

OEDIPUS

That he would not have said that I killed Laius
had he not met with you first.

CREON

You know yourself
whether he said this, but I demand that I
should hear as much from you as you from me.   575

OEDIPUS

Then hear—I'll not be proved a murderer.

CREON

Well, then. You're married to my sister?

OEDIPUS

Yes,
that I am not disposed to deny.

CREON

You rule
this country giving her an equal share
in the government?

OEDIPUS
    Yes, everything she wants
she has from me.   580

CREON
                    And I, as third with you,
    am rated as the equal of you both?

OEDIPUS
    Yes, and it's there you've proved yourself false friend.

CREON
    Not if you will reflect on it as I do.
    Consider, first, if you think anyone
    would choose to rule and fear rather than rule   585
    and sleep peacefully, if the power
    were equal in both cases. I, at least,
    I was not born with such a frantic yearning
    to be a king—but to do what kings do.
    And so it is with everyone who has learned
    wisdom and self-control. As it stands now,   590
    I get from you all the prizes—and without fear.
    But if I were the king myself, I must
    do much that went against the grain.
    How should despotic rule seem sweeter to me
    than painless power and an assured authority?
    I am not so deluded yet that I
    want other honors than those that come with profit.   595
    Now all men wish me joy; every man greets me;
    those who want things from you all fawn on me,
    success for them depends upon my favor.
    Why should I let all this go to win that?
    My mind would not be traitor if it's wise;°   600
    I am no treason lover, by my nature,
    nor could I ever bear to join a plot.
            Prove what I say. Go to the oracle

at Pytho and inquire about the answers,
if they are as I told you. For the rest,
if you discover I laid any plot   605
together with the seer, kill me, I say,
not only by your vote but by my own.
But do not charge me on obscure opinion
without some proof to back it. It's not just
lightly to count bad men as honest ones,   610
nor honest men as bad. To throw away
an honest friend is, as it were, to throw
your life away, which a man loves the best.
In time you'll know all this with certainty;
time is the only test of honest men,
one day is space enough to know who's bad.   615

CHORUS LEADER
His words are wise, king, for one who fears to fall.
Those who are quick of temper are not safe.

OEDIPUS
When he that plots against me secretly
moves quickly, I must quickly counterplot.
If I wait taking no decisive measure   620
his business will be done, and mine be spoiled.

CREON
What do you want to do then? Banish me?

OEDIPUS
No, certainly; kill you, not banish you.

CREON
I do not understand why you resent me so.°

. . . .

OEDIPUS
You speak as if you'll not listen nor obey.   625

CREON
I do not think that you've your wits about you.

OEDIPUS

For my own interests, yes.

CREON

But for mine, too,
you should think equally.

OEDIPUS

You are a traitor.

CREON

Suppose you do not understand?

OEDIPUS

But yet
I must be ruler.

CREON

Not if you rule badly.

OEDIPUS

O, city, city!

CREON

I too have some share   630
in the city; it is not yours alone.

CHORUS LEADER

Stop, my lords! Here—and in the nick of time
I see Jocasta coming from the house;
with her help settle the quarrel that now stirs you.

(Enter Jocasta, from the palace.)

JOCASTA

For shame! Why have you raised this foolish squabbling?
Are you not ashamed to air your private   635
troubles when the country's sick? Go inside, Oedipus,
and you, too, Creon, go to your house. Don't magnify
your nothing troubles.

CREON

       My sister: Oedipus,
your husband, thinks he has the right to do
terrible wrongs to me—he is choosing
between either banishing or killing me.°   640

OEDIPUS

He's right, Jocasta; for I find him plotting
with evil tricks against my person.

CREON

May never god bless me! May I die
accursed, if I've been guilty in any way
of any of the charges you bring against me!   645

JOCASTA

I beg you, Oedipus, trust him in this,
spare him for the sake of his oath to god,
for my sake, and the sake of those who stand here.

CHORUS [*singing in what follows, while Oedipus speaks*]

            STROPHE

Think carefully: be gracious, be merciful,
we beg of you.   650

OEDIPUS

In what would you have me yield?

CHORUS

He has never been foolish in the past.
He is strong in his oath now.
Spare him.

OEDIPUS

Do you know what you ask?

CHORUS

Yes.

OEDIPUS

Tell me then.   655

CHORUS

He has been your friend, he has sworn an oath; do not cast him
away dishonored on an obscure conjecture.

OEDIPUS

I would have you know that this request of yours
really requests my death or banishment.

CHORUS

May the sun god, king of gods, forbid! 660
May I die without god's blessing, without friends' help,
if I had any such thought.
But my spirit is broken by my unhappiness for my wasting country; 665
and this would but add troubles amongst ourselves to the other
troubles.

OEDIPUS

Well, let him go then—if I must die ten times for it,
or be sent out dishonored into exile. 670
It is your lips praying for him I pitied,
not his; wherever he is, I shall hate him.

CREON

I see you sulk in yielding and you're dangerous
when you are out of temper; natures like yours
are justly hardest for themselves to bear. 675

OEDIPUS

Leave me alone! Take yourself off, I tell you.

CREON

I'll go. You have not known me, but they have,
and they have known my innocence.

(Exit Creon, to the side.)

CHORUS [*singing in what follows, while Jocasta and Oedipus speak*]
                    ANTISTROPHE
Won't you take him inside, lady?

JOCASTA

Yes, when I've found out what was the matter. 680

CHORUS

There was some misconceived suspicion
of a story, and on the other side
the sting of injustice.

JOCASTA

So, on both sides?

CHORUS

Yes.

JOCASTA

What was the story?

CHORUS

I think it best, in the interests of our country, 685
to leave it where it ended.

OEDIPUS

You see where you have ended, straight of judgment
although you are, by softening my anger.

CHORUS

Sir, I have said before and I say again— 690
be sure that I would have been proved a madman,
bankrupt in sane council,
if I should put you away, you who steered the country I love safely
when it was crazed with troubles. God grant that now, too, 695
you may prove a fortunate guide for us.

JOCASTA

Tell me, my lord, I beg of you, what was it
that roused your anger so?

OEDIPUS

                                        Yes, I will tell you. 700
I honor you more than I honor them.
It was Creon and the plots he laid against me.

JOCASTA

Tell me—if you can clearly tell the quarrel—

OEDIPUS

Creon says that I'm the murderer of Laius.

JOCASTA

Of his own knowledge or on information?

OEDIPUS

He sent this rascal prophet to me, since   705
he keeps his own mouth clean of any guilt.

JOCASTA

Do not concern yourself about this matter;
listen to me and learn that human beings
have no part in the craft of prophecy.
Of that I'll show you a short proof.   710
There was an oracle once that came to Laius—
I will not say that it was Phoebus' own,
but it was from his servants—and it told him
that it was fate that he should die a victim
at the hands of his own son, a son to be born
of Laius and me. But, see now, he,
the king, was killed by foreign highway robbers   715
at a place where three roads meet—so goes the story;
and for the son—before three days were out
after his birth King Laius pierced his ankles
and by the hands of others cast him forth
upon a pathless hillside. So Apollo
failed to fulfill his oracle to the son,   720
that he should kill his father, and to Laius
also proved false in that the thing he feared,
death at his son's hands, never came to pass.
So clear in this case were the oracles,
describing the future. Give them no heed, I say;
what the god discovers need of, easily
he will show to us himself.   725

OEDIPUS

                     O dear Jocasta,
as I hear this from you, what wandering in my soul
now comes upon me—what turbulence of mind.

JOCASTA

What trouble is it, that you turn again
and speak like this?

OEDIPUS

                I thought I heard you say
that Laius was killed at a crossroads.   730

JOCASTA

Yes, that was how the story went and still
that word goes round.

OEDIPUS

             Where is this place, Jocasta,
where he was murdered?

JOCASTA

                  Phocis is the country
and the road splits there, one of two roads from Delphi,
another comes from Daulia.

OEDIPUS

                How long ago was this?   735

JOCASTA

The news came to the city just before
you became king and all men's eyes looked to you.
What is it, Oedipus, that's in your mind?

OEDIPUS

What have you designed, O Zeus, to do with me?

JOCASTA

What is the thought that troubles your heart?

OEDIPUS

  Don't ask me yet—tell me of Laius—   740
  How did he look? How old or young was he?

JOCASTA

  He was a tall man and his hair was grizzled
  already—partly white—and in his form
  not unlike you.

OEDIPUS

                  O god, I think I have
  called curses on myself in ignorance.   745

JOCASTA

  What do you mean? I'm frightened now, my king,
  when I look at you.

OEDIPUS

              I have a deadly fear
  that the old seer had eyes. You'll show me more
  if you can tell me one more thing.

JOCASTA

                  I will.
  I'm frightened—but you ask and I will listen,
  I'll tell you all I know.

OEDIPUS

             How was his company?   750
  Had he few with him when he went this journey,
  or many servants, as would suit a prince?

JOCASTA

  In all there were but five, and among them
  a herald; and one carriage for the king.

OEDIPUS

  It's plain—it's plain—who was it told you this?   755

JOCASTA

The only servant that escaped safe home.

OEDIPUS

Is he at home now?

JOCASTA

No, when he came home again
and saw that you were king and Laius dead,
he came to me and touched my hand and begged   760
that I should send him to the fields to be
my shepherd and so he might see the city
as far off as he could. So I
sent him away. He was an honest man,
as slaves go, and was worthy of far more
than what he asked of me.

OEDIPUS

So could he quickly now be brought back here?   765

JOCASTA

It can be done. Why is your heart so set on this?

OEDIPUS

O dear Jocasta, I am full of fears
that I have spoken far too much; and therefore
I wish to see this shepherd.

JOCASTA

He will come;
but, Oedipus, I think I too deserve
to know what is it that disquiets you.   770

OEDIPUS

It shall not be kept from you, since my mind
has gone so far with its forebodings. Whom
should I confide in rather than you? Who is there
of more importance to me who have passed
through such a fortune?
Polybus was my father, king of Corinth,

and Merope, the Dorian, my mother.   775
I was held greatest of the citizens
in Corinth till a curious chance befell me,
as I shall tell you—curious, indeed,
but hardly worth the store I set upon it.
There was a dinner and at it was a man,
a drunken man, who accused me in his drink
of being bastard. I was furious   780
but held my temper under for that day.
Next day I went and taxed my parents with it;
they took the insult ill and came down hard
on the man who had uttered it. So I
was comforted with regard to the two of them;   785
but still this thing rankled with me, for the story
kept on recurring. And so I went at last
to Pytho, though my parents did not know.
But Phoebus sent me home again unhonored
in what I came to learn, but he foretold
other and desperate horrors to befall me,   790
that I was fated to lie with my mother,
and show to daylight an accursed breed
which men would not endure, and I was doomed
to be murderer of the father that begot me.
        When I heard this I fled, and in the days
that followed I would measure from the stars   795
the whereabouts of Corinth—yes, I fled
to somewhere where I should not see fulfilled
the infamies told in that dreadful oracle.
And as I journeyed I came to the place
where, as you say, this king met with his death.
Jocasta, I will tell you the whole truth.   800
When I was near that branching of the crossroads,
going on foot, I was encountered by
a herald and a carriage with a man in it,
just as you tell me. He that led the way
and the old man himself wanted to thrust me   805

out of the road by force. I became angry
and struck the coachman who was pushing me.
When the old man saw this he waited for his chance,
and as I passed he struck me from his carriage,
full on the head with his two-pointed goad.
He paid for this in full, and more: my stick   810
quickly struck him backward from the car
and he rolled out of it. And then I killed them
all. If it happens there was any tie
of kinship between this man and Laius,
who is there now more miserable than I,   815
what man on earth so hated by the gods,
since neither citizen nor foreigner
may welcome me at home or even greet me,
but drive me out of doors? And it is I,
I and no other have so cursed myself.   820
And I pollute the bed of him I killed
by the hands that killed him. Was I not born evil?
Am I not utterly unclean, if I have to flee
and in my banishment not even see
my kindred nor set foot in my own country,
or otherwise my fate is to be yoked   825
in marriage with my mother and kill my father,
Polybus who begot me and who reared me?
Would not one rightly judge and say that on me
these things were sent by some malignant god?
O no, no, no—O holy majesty   830
of god on high, may I not see that day!
May I be gone out of men's sight before
I see the deadly taint of this disaster
come upon me.

CHORUS LEADER
    My lord, we fear this too. But till this man
    is here and you have heard his story, hope.   835

OEDIPUS

   Yes, I have just this much of hope as well:
to wait until the herdsman comes.

JOCASTA

                 And what
will you want with him, once he has appeared?

OEDIPUS

   I'll tell you; if I find that his story is
the same as yours, I will be clear of guilt.   840

JOCASTA

   What in particular did you learn from my story?

OEDIPUS

   You said that he spoke of highway robbers who
killed Laius. Now if he still uses that
same number, I was not the one who killed him.
One man cannot be the same as many.
But if he speaks clearly of one man on his own,   845
indeed the guilty balance tilts toward me.

JOCASTA

   Be sure, at least, that this was how he told the story;
and he cannot unsay this now, for everyone
in the city heard it—not just I alone.   850
But even if he turns from what he said then,
not ever will he prove, my lord, that rightly
the murder of Laius squares with Apollo's words,
Apollo, who declared that by his son
from me he would be killed. And yet
that poor creature surely did not kill him—   855
for he himself died first. As far as prophecy
goes, henceforward I won't look to the right
nor to the left hand either.

OEDIPUS

Your opinion's sound. But yet, send someone for   860
the peasant to bring him here; do not neglect it.

JOCASTA

I will send, and quickly. Now let us go indoors.
I will do nothing except what pleases you.

(Exit, into the palace.)

CHORUS [*singing*]

STROPHE A

May destiny ever find me
pious in word and deed
prescribed by the laws that live on high: 865
laws begotten in the clear air of heaven,
whose only father is Olympus;
no mortal nature brought them to birth,
no forgetfulness shall lull them to sleep;   870
for god is great in them and grows not old.

ANTISTROPHE A

Insolence breeds the tyrant, insolence
if it is glutted with a surfeit, unseasonable, unprofitable,
climbs to the rooftop and plunges   875
sheer down to the ruin that must be,
and there its feet are no service.
But I pray that the god may never   880
abolish the eager ambition that profits the state.
For I shall never cease to hold the god as our protector.

STROPHE B

If a man walks with haughtiness
of hand or word and gives no heed   885
to Justice and the shrines of gods
despises—may an evil doom
smite him for his ill-starred pride of heart!—
if he reaps gains without justice
and will not hold from impiety   890

and his fingers itch for untouchable things.
When such things are done, what man shall contrive
to shield his life from the shafts of the god?
When such deeds are held in honor,   895
why should I honor the gods in the dance?

ANTISTROPHE B
No longer to the holy place,
to the navel of earth I'll go
to worship, nor to Abae   900
nor to Olympia,
unless the oracles are proved to fit,
for all men's hands to point at.
O Zeus, if you are rightly called
the sovereign lord, all-mastering,
let this not escape you nor your ever-living power!   905
The oracles concerning Laius
are old and dim and men regard them not.
Apollo is nowhere clear in honor; the gods' service perishes.   910

(Enter Jocasta from the palace, carrying garlands.)

JOCASTA
Lords of the land, I have had the thought to go
to the gods' temples, bringing in my hand
garlands and gifts of incense, as you see.
For Oedipus excites himself too much
with all kinds of worries, not conjecturing,   915
like a man of sense, what will be from what was,
but he is always at the speaker's mercy,
when he speaks terrors. I can do no good
by my advice, and so I come as suppliant
to you, Lycian Apollo, who are nearest.   920
These are the symbols of my prayer and this
my prayer: grant us escape free of the curse.
Now when we look to him we are all afraid;
he's pilot of our ship and he is frightened.

(Enter Messenger, from the side.)

MESSENGER

    Might I learn from you, sirs, where is the house of Oedipus?   925
    Or better, if you know, where is the king himself?

CHORUS LEADER

    This is his house and he is within; the lady
    here is his wife and mother of his children.

MESSENGER

    God bless you, lady! God bless your household too!
    God bless the noble wife of Oedipus!   930

JOCASTA

    And god bless you, sir, for your kind greeting!
    What do you want of us that you have come here?
    What have you to tell us?

MESSENGER

              Good news, lady.
    Good for your house and also for your husband.

JOCASTA

    What is your news? And who sent you to us?   935

MESSENGER

    I come from Corinth; the news I bring will give you
    pleasure, for sure. Perhaps some pain as well.

JOCASTA

    What is it, then, this news of double meaning?

MESSENGER

    The people of the Isthmus will choose Oedipus
    to be their king. That is the rumor there.   940

JOCASTA

    But isn't their king still aged Polybus?

MESSENGER

    No. He is in his grave. Death has got him.

JOCASTA

Is that the truth? Is Oedipus' father dead?

MESSENGER

May I die myself if it be otherwise!

JOCASTA   *(To a servant.)*

Be quick and run to tell the king the news!   945
O oracles of the gods, where are you now?
It was from this man Oedipus fled, long ago,
lest he should be his murderer! And now, by chance,
he is dead, in the course of nature, not killed by him.

(Enter Oedipus from the palace.)

OEDIPUS

Dearest Jocasta, why have you sent for me?   950

JOCASTA

Listen to this man and when you hear, reflect
on what the god's holy oracles have come to.

OEDIPUS

Who is he? What is his message for me?

JOCASTA

He comes from Corinth and tells us that your father   955
Polybus is no more, but dead and gone.

OEDIPUS

What's this you say, stranger? Tell me yourself.

MESSENGER

If this is what you first want clearly told:
be sure, Polybus has gone down to death.

OEDIPUS

Was it by treachery, or from sickness?   960

MESSENGER

A small thing will put old bodies asleep.

OEDIPUS

So he died of sickness, it seems—poor old man!

MESSENGER

Yes, and of age—the long years he had measured.

OEDIPUS

Ah! Ah! O dear Jocasta, why should one
look to the Pythian hearth? Why should one look   965
to the birds screaming overhead? They prophesied
that I should kill my father! But he's dead,
and hidden deep in earth, and I stand here
who never laid a hand on spear against him —
unless perhaps he died of longing for me,
and thus I am his murderer. But they,   970
the oracles, as they stand—he's taken them
away with him, they're dead as he himself is,
and worthless.

JOCASTA

                    That I already told you before now.

OEDIPUS

You did, but I was misled by my fear.

JOCASTA

Then lay no more of them to heart, not one.   975

OEDIPUS

But surely I must fear my mother's bed?

JOCASTA

Why should man fear since chance is all in all
for him, and he can clearly foreknow nothing?
Best to live lightly, as one can, unthinkingly.
As to your mother's marriage bed—do not   980
feel fear about this: before now, many a man
in his dreams has lain with his own mother.
But he to whom such things are nothing bears
his life most easily.

OEDIPUS

All that you say would be said perfectly
if she were dead; but since she lives I must   985
still fear, although you talk so well, Jocasta.

JOCASTA

Still in your father's death there's light of comfort?

OEDIPUS

Great light of comfort; but I fear the living.

MESSENGER

Who is the woman that makes you afraid?

OEDIPUS

Merope, old man, Polybus' wife.   990

MESSENGER

What about her frightens the queen and you?

OEDIPUS

A terrible oracle, stranger, from the gods.

MESSENGER

Can it be told? Or does the sacred law
forbid another to have knowledge of it?

OEDIPUS

O no! Once on a time Loxias said
that I should lie with my own mother and   995
take on my hands the blood of my own father.
And so for these long years I've lived away
from Corinth; it has been to my good fortune;
but yet it's sweet to see the face of parents.

MESSENGER

This was the fear that drove you out of Corinth?   1000

OEDIPUS

Old man, I did not wish to kill my father.

MESSENGER

Why should I not free you from this fear, sir,
since I have come to you in all goodwill?

OEDIPUS

You would not find me thankless if you did.

MESSENGER

Why, it was just for this I brought the news—   1005
to earn your thanks when you had come safe home.

OEDIPUS

No, I will never come near my parents.

MESSENGER

                    Son,
it's very plain you don't know what you're doing.

OEDIPUS

What do you mean, old man? For god's sake, tell me.

MESSENGER

If your homecoming is checked by fears like these.   1010

OEDIPUS

Yes, I'm afraid that Phoebus may prove right.

MESSENGER

Pollution from your parents?

OEDIPUS

                    Yes, old man;
that is my constant terror.

MESSENGER

                    Do you know
that all your fears are empty?

OEDIPUS

                    How is that,
if they are father and mother and I their son?   1015

MESSENGER
Because Polybus was no kin to you in blood.

OEDIPUS
What, was not Polybus my father?

MESSENGER
No more than I but just so much.

OEDIPUS
     How can
my father be my father as much as one
that's nothing to me?

MESSENGER
    Neither he nor I   1020
begot you.

OEDIPUS
        Why then did he call me son?

MESSENGER
A gift he took you from these hands of mine.

OEDIPUS
Did he love so much what he took from another's hand?

MESSENGER
His childlessness before persuaded him.

OEDIPUS
Was I a child you bought or found when I   1025
was given to him?

MESSENGER
       On Cithaeron's slopes
in the twisting thickets you were found.

OEDIPUS
       And why
were you a traveler in those parts?

MESSENGER

I was
in charge of mountain flocks.

OEDIPUS

You were a shepherd?
A hireling vagrant?

MESSENGER

Yes, but at least at that time   1030
the man that saved your life, son.

OEDIPUS

What ailed me when you took me in your arms?

MESSENGER

In that your ankles should be witnesses.

OEDIPUS

Why do you speak of that old pain?

MESSENGER

I loosed you;
the tendons of your feet were pierced and fettered—   1035

OEDIPUS

My swaddling clothes brought me a rare disgrace.

MESSENGER

so that from this you're called your present name.

OEDIPUS

Was this my father's doing or my mother's?
For god's sake, tell me.

MESSENGER

I don't know, but he
who gave you to me has more knowledge than I.

OEDIPUS

You yourself did not find me then? You took me
from someone else?

MESSENGER

Yes, from another shepherd.

OEDIPUS

Who was he? Do you know him well enough
to tell?

MESSENGER

He was called one of Laius' men.

OEDIPUS

You mean the king who reigned here in the old days?

MESSENGER

Yes, he was that man's shepherd.

OEDIPUS

Is he alive
still, so that I could see him?

MESSENGER

You who live here
would know that best.

OEDIPUS

Do any of you here
know of this shepherd whom he speaks about
in town or in the fields? Tell me. It's time
that this was found out once for all.

CHORUS LEADER

I think he is none other than the peasant
whom you have sought to see already; but
Jocasta here can tell us best of that.

OEDIPUS

Jocasta, do you know about this man
whom we have sent for? Is that the man he mentions?

JOCASTA

Why ask of whom he spoke? Don't give it heed;

nor try to keep in mind what has been said.
It will be wasted labor.

OEDIPUS
                    With such clues
I could not fail to bring my birth to light.

JOCASTA
I beg you—do not hunt this out—I beg you,   1060
if you have any care for your own life.
What I am suffering is enough.

OEDIPUS
                              Keep up
your heart, Jocasta. Though I'm proved a slave,
thrice slave, and though my mother be thrice slave,
you'll not be shown to be of lowly lineage.

JOCASTA
O be persuaded by me, I entreat you;
do not do this.

OEDIPUS
I will not be persuaded to let be   1065
the chance of finding out the whole thing clearly.

JOCASTA
It is because I wish you well that I
give you this counsel—and it's the best counsel.

OEDIPUS
Then the best counsel vexes me, and has
for some while since.

JOCASTA
                    O Oedipus, god help you!
God keep you from the knowledge of who you are!

OEDIPUS
Here, someone, go and fetch the shepherd for me;
and let her find her joy in her rich family!   1070

JOCASTA

O Oedipus, unhappy Oedipus!
that is all I can call you, and the last thing
that I shall ever call you.

(Exit Jocasta into the palace.)

CHORUS LEADER

Why has the queen gone, Oedipus, in wild
grief rushing from us? I am afraid that trouble
will break out of this silence.   1075

OEDIPUS

Break out what will! I at least shall be
willing to see my ancestry, though humble.
Perhaps she is ashamed of my low birth,
for she has all a woman's high-flown pride.
But I account myself a child of Fortune,   1080
beneficent goddess, and I shall not be
dishonored. Fortune's the mother from whom I spring;
the months, my brothers, marked me, now as small,
and now again as mighty. Such is my breeding,
and I shall never prove so false to it,
as not to find the secret of my birth.   1085

CHORUS [*singing*]

STROPHE

If I am a prophet and wise of heart
you shall not fail, Cithaeron,
by the limitless sky, you shall not!—
to know that tomorrow's full moon   1090
shall honor you as Oedipus' compatriot,
his mother and nurse at once;
and that you shall be honored in dancing by us,
for rendering service to our king.   1095
Apollo, to whom we cry, find these things pleasing!

ANTISTROPHE

Who was it bore you, child? One of

the long-lived nymphs who lay with Pan—   1100
the father who treads the hills?
Or was your mother a bride of Loxias? The grassy slopes
are all of them dear to him. Or perhaps Cyllene's king
or the Bacchants' god that lives on the tops   1105
of the hills received you, a gift from some
one of the dark-eyed Nymphs, with whom he mostly plays?

(Enter an old Herdsman from the side, led by Oedipus' servants.)

OEDIPUS

If someone like myself who never met him   1110
may make a guess—I think this is the herdsman,
whom we were seeking. His old age is consonant
with the other's. And besides, the men who bring him
I recognize as my own servants. But you
perhaps may better me in knowledge since   1115
you've seen the man before.

CHORUS LEADER

                You can be sure
I recognize him. For if Laius
had ever an honest shepherd, this was he.

OEDIPUS

You, sir, from Corinth, I must ask you first,
is this the man you spoke of?

MESSENGER

              This is he   1120
before your eyes.

OEDIPUS

             Old man, look here at me
and tell me what I ask you. Were you ever
a servant of King Laius?

HERDSMAN

         I was—
no slave he bought but reared in his own house.

OEDIPUS
What did you do as work? How did you live?

HERDSMAN
Most of my life was spent among the flocks.   1125

OEDIPUS
In what part of the country did you live?

HERDSMAN
Cithaeron and the places near to it.

OEDIPUS
And somewhere there perhaps you knew this man?

HERDSMAN
What was he doing? What man?

OEDIPUS
                              This man here,
have you had any dealings with him?   1130

HERDSMAN
                    No—
not such that I can quickly call to mind.

MESSENGER
That is no wonder, master. But I'll help him
remember what he does not know. For I know
that he knows well the country of Cithaeron,
how he with two flocks, I with one, together   1135
kept company for three years—six months each year—
from spring till autumn time. When winter came
I drove my flocks back to our fold, back home,
while this man, he drove his to Laius' steadings.
Am I right or not in what I say we did?   1140

HERDSMAN
You're right—although it's a long time ago.

MESSENGER

Do you remember giving me a baby
to bring up as my foster child?

HERDSMAN

What's this?
Why do you ask this question?

MESSENGER

Look old man,
here he is—here's the man who was that child!   1145

HERDSMAN

Death take you! Won't you hold your tongue?

OEDIPUS

No, no,
do not find fault with him, old man. Your words
are more at fault than his.

HERDSMAN

O best of masters,
how do I give offense?

OEDIPUS

When you refuse
to speak about the child of whom he asks you.   1150

HERDSMAN

He speaks out of his ignorance, without meaning.

OEDIPUS

If you'll not talk to gratify me, you
will talk with pain to urge you.

HERDSMAN

O please, sir,
don't hurt an old man, sir.

OEDIPUS   *(To the servants.)*

Here, one of you,
twist his hands behind him.

HERDSMAN

                              Why, god help me, why?
What do you want to know?   1155

OEDIPUS

                              You gave a child
to him—the child he asked you of?

HERDSMAN

                              I did.
I wish I'd died the day I did.

OEDIPUS

                    You will
unless you tell me truly.

HERDSMAN

                              And I'll die
far worse if I should tell you.

OEDIPUS

                              This fellow   1160
is bent on more delays, as it would seem.

HERDSMAN

O no, no! I have told you that I gave it.

OEDIPUS

Where did you get this child from? Was it your own
or did you get it from another?

HERDSMAN

                    Not
my own at all; I had it from someone.

OEDIPUS

One of these citizens? And from what house?

HERDSMAN

O master, please—I beg you, master, please   1165
don't ask me more.

OEDIPUS

You're a dead man if I

ask you again.

HERDSMAN

The child came from the house

of Laius.

OEDIPUS

A slave? Or born from himself?

HERDSMAN

O god, I am on the brink of frightful speech.

OEDIPUS

And I of frightful hearing. But I must hear.   1170

HERDSMAN

The child was called his child; but she within,
your wife would tell you best how all this was.

OEDIPUS

She gave it to you?

HERDSMAN

Yes she did, my lord.

OEDIPUS

To do what with it?

HERDSMAN

Make away with it.

OEDIPUS

She was so hard—its mother?   1175

HERDSMAN

Aye, through fear

of evil oracles.

OEDIPUS

Which?

HERDSMAN

They said that he
should kill his parents.

OEDIPUS

How was it that you
gave it away to this old man?

HERDSMAN

O master,
I pitied it, and thought that I could send it
off to another country: and this man
was from another country. But he saved it   1180
for the most terrible troubles. If you are
the man he says you are, you're bred to misery.

OEDIPUS

O, O, O, they will all come,
all come out clearly! Light of the sun, let me
look upon you no more after today!
I who first saw the light bred of a coupling
accursed, and accursed in my living
with them I lived with, cursed in my killing.   1185

(Exit Oedipus into the palace. All but the Chorus depart to the side.)

CHORUS [*singing*]

STROPHE A

O generations of men, how I
count you as equal with those who live
not at all!
What man, what man on earth wins more   1190
of happiness than a seeming
and after that falling away?
Oedipus, you are my pattern of this,
Oedipus, you and your fate!   1195
Luckless Oedipus, as I look at you,
I count nothing in human affairs happy.

Inasmuch as you shot your bolt
beyond the others and won the prize
of happiness complete—
O Zeus—and killed and reduced to naught
the hooked taloned maid of the riddling speech,   1200
standing a tower against death for my land;
hence you are called my king and hence
have been honored the highest of all
honors; and hence you ruled
in the great city of Thebes.

But now whose tale is more miserable?
Who is there lives with a savager fate?°   1205
Whose troubles so reverse his life as his?
O Oedipus, the famous prince
for whom the same great harbor
the same both for father and son
sufficed for bridal bed,   1210
how, O how, have the furrows ploughed
by your father endured to bear you, poor wretch,
and remain silent so long?

Time who sees all has found you out
against your will; judges your marriage accursed,
begetter and begotten at one in it.   1215
O child of Laius,
would I had never seen you.
I weep for you and cry
a dirge of lamentation.
To speak directly, I drew my breath   1220
from you at the first and so now I lull
my eyes to sleep with your name.

(Enter a Second Messenger, from the palace.)

SECOND MESSENGER

    O princes always honored by our country,
what deeds you'll hear of and what horrors see,
what grief you'll feel, if you as trueborn Thebans   1225
care for the house of Labdacus's sons.
No river, not Phasis nor Ister, can purge this house,
I think, with all their streams, such things
it hides, such evils shortly will bring forth
into the light, evils done on purpose;   1230
and troubles hurt the most
when they prove self-inflicted.

CHORUS LEADER

    What we had known before did not fall short
of bitter groaning; now what's more to tell?

SECOND MESSENGER

    Shortest to hear and say—our glorious queen
Jocasta's dead.   1235

CHORUS LEADER

            Unhappy woman! How?

SECOND MESSENGER

    By her own hand. You're spared the greatest pain
of what was done—you did not see the sight.
Yet insofar as I remember it
you'll hear the sufferings of our unlucky queen.   1240
        When she came raging into the house she went
straight to her marriage bed, tearing her hair
with both her hands, and slammed the bedroom doors
behind her shut, crying upon Laius
long dead—"Do you remember, Laius,   1245
that night long past which bred a child for us
to send you to your death and leave
a mother making children with her son?"
And then she groaned and cursed the bed in which
she brought forth husband by her husband, children   1250

by her own child, an infamous double bond.
    How after that she died I do not know—
for Oedipus distracted us from seeing.
He burst upon us shouting and we looked
to him as he paced frantically around,
begging us always: "Give me a sword, I say,   1255
to find this wife no wife, this mother's womb,
this field of double sowing whence I sprang
and where I sowed my children!" As he raved
some god showed him the way—none of us there.
Bellowing terribly and led by some   1260
invisible guide he rushed on the two doors—
wrenching the bending bolts out of their sockets,
he charged inside. There, there, we saw his wife
hanging, the twisted rope around her neck.
When he saw her, he cried out fearfully   1265
and cut the dangling noose. Then, as she lay,
poor woman, on the ground, what happened after,
was terrible to see. He tore the brooches—
the gold chased brooches fastening her robe—
away from her and lifting them up high
dashed them on his own eyeballs, shrieking out   1270
such things as: "You will never see the crime
I have committed or had done upon me!
Dark eyes, now in the days to come look on
forbidden faces, do not recognize
those whom you long for"—with such imprecations
he struck his eyes again and yet again   1275
with the brooches. And the bleeding eyeballs gushed
and stained his cheeks—no sluggish oozing drops
but a black rain and bloody hail poured down.
    So it has broken—and not on one head alone°   1280
but troubles mixed for husband and for wife.
The fortune of the days gone by was true
good fortune—but today groans and destruction

and death and shame—of all ills that can be named
not one is missing.   1285

CHORUS LEADER
  Is he now in any ease from pain?

SECOND MESSENGER
              He shouts
  for someone to unbar the doors and show him
  to all the men of Thebes, his father's killer,
  his mother's—no I cannot say the word,
  it is unholy—for he'll cast himself,   1290
  out of the land, he says, and not remain
  to bring a curse upon his house, the curse
  he called upon it in his proclamation. But
  he wants for strength, aye, and someone to guide him;
  his sickness is too great to bear. You, too,
  will be shown that. The bolts are opening.
  Soon you will see a sight to waken pity   1295
  even in one who feels disgust or hatred.

                    (Enter the blinded Oedipus, from the palace.)

CHORUS [*chanting*]
  This is a terrible sight for men to see!
  I never encountered a worse horror!
  Poor wretch, what madness came upon you?   1300
  What evil spirit leaped upon your life
  to your ill luck—a leap beyond man's strength!
  Indeed I pity you, but I cannot
  look at you, though there's much I want to ask
  and much to learn and much to see.   1305
  I shudder at the sight of you.

OEDIPUS [*singing in what follows, while the Chorus speaks*]
  O, O,
  where am I going? Where is my voice

borne on the wind to and fro? 1310
Spirit, how far have you sprung?

CHORUS LEADER

To a terrible place which men's ears
may not hear of, nor their eyes see it.

OEDIPUS

STROPHE A

Darkness!
Horror of darkness enfolding, resistless, unspeakable visitant sped 1315
by an ill wind in haste!°
Madness and stabbing pain and memory
of my evils!

CHORUS LEADER

In such misfortunes it's no wonder
if double weighs the burden of your grief. 1320

OEDIPUS

ANTISTROPHE A

My friend,
you are the only one steadfast, the only one that attends on me;
you still stay nursing the blind man.
Your care is not unnoticed. I recognize 1325
your voice, although this darkness is my world.

CHORUS LEADER

Doer of dreadful deeds, how did you dare
so far to do despite to your own eyes?
What spirit urged you to it?

OEDIPUS

STROPHE B

It was Apollo, friends, Apollo,
that brought this bitter bitterness, my sorrows to completion. 1330
But the hand that struck me
was none but my own.
Why should I see
whose vision showed me nothing sweet to see? 1335

CHORUS [*now singing*]
  These things are as you say.

OEDIPUS
  What can I see to love?
  What greeting can touch my ears with joy?
  Take me away, and haste—to a place out of the way!   1340
  Take me away, my friends, the greatly miserable,
  the most accursed, whom the gods too hate   1345
  above all men on earth!

CHORUS LEADER
  Unhappy in your mind and your misfortune,
  would I had never known you!

OEDIPUS
                    ANTISTROPHE B
  Curse on the man° who took
  the cruel bonds from off my legs, as I lay there.   1350
  He stole me from death and saved me,
  no kindly service.
  Had I died then,
  I would not be so burdensome to friends or to myself.   1355

CHORUS
  I, too, could have wished it had been so.

OEDIPUS
  Then I would not have come
  to kill my father and marry my mother infamously.
  Now I am godless and child of impurity,   1360
  begetter in the same seed that created my wretched self.
  If there is any ill worse than ill,   1365
  that is the lot of Oedipus.

CHORUS LEADER
  I cannot say your remedy was good;
  you would be better dead than blind and living.

OEDIPUS [*now speaking*]

What I have done here was best done—don't tell me
otherwise, do not give me further counsel.   1370
I do not know with what eyes I could look
upon my father when I die and go
under the earth, nor yet my wretched mother—
those two to whom I have done things deserving
worse punishment than hanging. Would the sight
of children, bred as mine are, gladden me?   1375
No, not these eyes, never. And my city,
its towers and sacred places of the gods,
where I was raised as the noblest man in Thebes,   1380
of these I robbed my miserable self
when I commanded all to drive him out,
the criminal since proved by the gods impure
and of the race of Laius.
To this guilt I bore witness against myself—
with what eyes was I to look upon my people?   1385
No. If there were a means to choke the fountain
of hearing I would not have stayed my hand
from locking up my miserable carcass,
seeing and hearing nothing; it is sweet
to keep our thoughts out of the range of hurt.   1390
        Cithaeron, why did you receive me? Why
having received me did you not kill me straight?
And so I'd not have shown to men my birth.
O Polybus and Corinth and the house,
the old house that I used to call my father's—   1395
what fairness you were nurse to, and what foulness
festered beneath! Now I am found to be
evil and a son of evil. Crossroads,
and hidden glade, oak and the narrow way
at the crossroads that drank my father's blood—   1400
my own blood—from my hands, do you remember
still what I did as you looked on, and what
I did when I came here? O marriage, marriage!

you bred me and again when you had bred
you produced the same seed again and displayed to men   1405
fathers, brothers, children, an incestuous brood,
brides, wives, and mothers, all the foulest deeds
that can be in this world of ours.
     Come—it's unfit to say what is unfit
to do.—I beg of you in the gods' name hide me   1410
somewhere outside your country, yes, or kill me,
or throw me into the sea, to be forever
out of your sight. Approach and deign to touch me
for all my wretchedness, and do not fear.
No man but I can bear my evil doom.   1415

(Enter Creon, from the side, with attendants.)

CHORUS LEADER
Here Creon comes in fit time to perform
or give advice in what you ask of us.
Creon is left sole ruler in your stead.

OEDIPUS
Creon! Creon! What shall I say to him?
How can I justly hope that he will trust me?   1420
In what is past I have been proved toward him
an utter liar.

CREON
                    Oedipus, I've come
not so that I might laugh at you nor taunt you
with evil of the past.

(To attendants.)

                    But even if you men
have no more shame before the face of men,
reverence at least the flame that gives all life,   1425
our lord the Sun, and do not show unveiled
to him pollution such that neither land
nor holy rain nor light of day can welcome.

Be quick and take him in. It is most decent
that only kin should see and hear the troubles   1430
of kin.

OEDIPUS
                              I beg you, since you've torn me from
my dreadful expectations and have come
in a most noble spirit to a man
that has used you vilely—do a thing for me.
I shall speak for your own good, not for my own.

CREON
What do you need that you would ask of me?   1435

OEDIPUS
Drive me from here with all the speed you can
to where I may not hear a human voice.

CREON
Be sure, I would have done this had not I
wished first of all to learn from the god the course
of action I should follow.

OEDIPUS
                                      But his word   1440
has been quite clear to let the parricide,
the sinner, die.

CREON
                              Yes, that indeed was said.
But in the present need we had best discover
what we should do.

OEDIPUS
                              And will you ask about
a man so wretched?

CREON
                              Now even you will trust   1445
the god.

OEDIPUS

So. I command you—and will beseech you—
to her that lies inside that house give burial
as you would have it; she is yours and rightly
you will perform the rites for her. For me—
never let this my father's city have me   1450
living a dweller in it. Leave me live
in the mountains where Cithaeron is that's called
my mountain, which my mother and my father
while they were living would have made my tomb.
So I may die by their decree who sought
indeed to kill me. Yet I know this much: 1455
no sickness and no other thing will kill me.
I would not have been saved from death if not
for some strange evil fate. Well, let my fate
go where it will.

Creon, you need not care
about my sons; they're men and so wherever   1460
they are, they will not lack a livelihood.
But my two girls—so sad and pitiful—
whose table never stood apart from mine,
and everything I touched they always shared—   1465
O Creon, have a thought for them! And most
I wish that you might allow me to touch them
and sorrow with them.

(Enter Antigone and Ismene from the palace.)

O my lord! O true noble Creon! May I
really touch them, as when I saw?   1470
What shall I say?
Can I hear them sobbing—my two darlings!—
and Creon has had pity and has sent me
what I loved most?
Am I right?   1475

CREON

You're right: it was I gave you this

because I knew from old days how you loved them
as I see now.

OEDIPUS

God bless you for it, Creon,
and may god guard you better on your road
than he did me!
                                    O children,
where are you? Come here, come to my hands,   1480
a brother's hands which turned your father's eyes,
those bright eyes you knew once, to what you see,
a father seeing nothing, knowing nothing,
begetting you from his own source of life.   1485
I weep for you—I cannot see your faces—
I weep when I think of the bitterness
there will be in your lives, how you must live
before the world. At what assemblages
of citizens will you attend? To what
festivals will you go and not come home   1490
in tears instead of sharing in the holiday?
And when you're ripe for marriage, who will he be,
the man who'll risk to take such infamy
as shall cling to my children, to bring hurt
on them and those that marry with them? What   1495
evil is not there? "Your father killed his father
and sowed the seed where he had sprung himself
and begot you out of the womb that held him."
Such insults you will hear. Then who will marry you?   1500
No one, my children; clearly you are doomed
to waste away in barrenness unmarried.
          Son of Menoeceus, since you are all the father
left these two girls, and we, their parents, both
are dead to them—do not allow them to wander   1505
like beggars, poor and husbandless.
They are of your own blood.
And do not make them equal with myself

in wretchedness; for you can see them now
so young, so utterly alone, save for you only.
Touch my hand, noble Creon, and say yes.   1510
    If you were older, children, and were wiser,
there's much advice I'd give you. But as it is,
let this be what you pray: to find a life
wherever there is opportunity
to live, a better life than was your father's.

CREON

Your tears have had enough of scope; now go within the
    house.   1515

OEDIPUS

I must obey, though bitter of heart.

CREON

                    In season, all is good.

OEDIPUS

Do you know on what conditions I obey?

CREON

                              You tell me them,
and I shall know them when I hear.

OEDIPUS

                    That you shall send me out
to live away from Thebes.

CREON

                    That gift you must ask of the god.

OEDIPUS

But I'm now hated by the gods.

CREON

                    So quickly you'll obtain your prayer.

OEDIPUS

You consent then?   1520

CREON
                    What I do not mean, I do not use to say.

OEDIPUS
    Now lead me away from here.

CREON
                    Let go the children, then, and come.

OEDIPUS
    Do not take them from me.

CREON
                    Do not seek to be master in everything,
        for the things you mastered did not follow you throughout
            your life.

                                    (*Creon and Oedipus depart.*)

CHORUS°
    You that live in my ancestral Thebes, behold this Oedipus—
    him who knew the famous riddles and was a man most
        masterful;   1525
    not a citizen who did not look with envy on his lot—
    see him now and see the breakers of misfortune swallow him!
    Look upon that last day always. Count no mortal happy till
    he has passed the final limit of his life secure from pain.   1530

OEDIPUS AT COLONUS

Translated by ROBERT FITZGERALD

OEDIPUS AT COLONUS

Characters   OEDIPUS
                  ANTIGONE, daughter of Oedipus
                  A STRANGER
                  CHORUS of old men of Colonus
                  ISMENE, daughter of Oedipus
                  THESEUS, king of Athens
                  CREON, king of Thebes
                  POLYNICES, son of Oedipus
                  A MESSENGER

Scene: *A grove in Colonus dedicated to the Furies. A statue or stele of the legendary horseman-hero Colonus can be seen on one side. There is a flat rock, sacred throne of the Furies, in the middle of the orchestra, and another low outcrop of rock to one side.*

    (*Enter Oedipus from one side, old, blind, and ragged, led by Antigone.*)

OEDIPUS
  My daughter—daughter of the blind old man—
  where have we come to now, Antigone?
  What lands are these, or holdings of what city?
  Who will be kind to Oedipus this evening°
  and give alms to the wanderer?
  Though he ask little and receive still less,   5
  it is sufficient:
                suffering and time,
  vast time, have been instructors in contentment,
  which kingliness° teaches too.

But now, child,
if you can see a resting place—perhaps
a roadside fountain, or some holy grove,   10
tell me and let me pause there and sit down:
so we may learn our whereabouts, and take
our cue from what we hear, as strangers should.

ANTIGONE

Father, poor tired Oedipus, the towers
that crown the city still seem far away;   15
as for this place, it is clearly a holy one,
shady with vines and olive trees and laurel;
a covert for the song and hush of nightingales
in their snug wings.
                    But rest on this rough stone.
It was a long road for an old man to travel.   20

OEDIPUS

Help me sit down; take care of the blind man.

ANTIGONE

After so long, you need not tell me, father.

                (Antigone helps Oedipus sit down on the rock, at center.)

OEDIPUS

What can you say, now, as to where we are?

ANTIGONE

This place I do not know; I know the city
must be Athens.

OEDIPUS

                As all the travelers said.   25

ANTIGONE

Then shall I go and ask what place this is?

OEDIPUS

Do, child, if there is any life nearby.

ANTIGONE

Oh, but indeed there is; I need not leave you;
I see a man, now, not far away from us.

OEDIPUS

Is he coming this way? Has he started toward us?   30

(Enter a Stranger, from the side.)

ANTIGONE

Here he is now.
                         Say what seems best to you,
father; the man is here.

OEDIPUS

Friend, my daughter's eyes serve for my own.
She tells me we are fortunate enough to meet you;
and no doubt you will inform us—   35

STRANGER

                         Do not go on!
First, move from where you sit; the place is holy;
it is forbidden to walk upon that ground.

OEDIPUS

What ground is this? What god is honored here?

STRANGER

It is not to be touched, no one may live upon it;
most dreadful are its divinities, most feared,
Daughters of Darkness and mysterious Earth.   40

OEDIPUS

Under what solemn name shall I invoke them?

STRANGER

The people here prefer to address them as Gentle
All-Seeing Ones; elsewhere there are other names.

OEDIPUS

Then may they be gentle to the suppliant;
for I shall never leave this resting place.   45

STRANGER

What is the meaning of this?

OEDIPUS

It was ordained;
I recognize it now.

STRANGER

Without authority
from the city government I dare not move you;
first I must show them what you are doing.

OEDIPUS

Friend, in the name of god, bear with me now!
I turn to you for light; answer the wanderer.°   50

STRANGER

Speak. You will have no discourtesy from me.

OEDIPUS

What is this region that we two have entered?

STRANGER

As much as I can tell you, I will tell.
This country, all of it, is blessed ground;
the god Poseidon loves it; in it the fire carrier
Prometheus has his influence; in particular   55
that spot you rest on has been called this earth's
Doorsill of Brass, and buttress of great Athens.
All men of this land claim descent from him
who is sculptured here, Colonus master horseman,
and bear his name in common with their own.   60
That is this country, stranger: honored less
in histories than in the hearts of the people.

OEDIPUS

Then people live here on their lands?

STRANGER

They do,
the clan of those descended from that hero.   65

OEDIPUS
  Ruled by a prince? Or by the greater number?

STRANGER
  The land is governed from Athens, by the king.

OEDIPUS
  And who is he whose word has power here?

STRANGER
  Theseus, son of Aegeus, the king before him.

OEDIPUS
  Ah. Would someone then go to this king for me?   70

STRANGER
  To tell him what? Perhaps to urge his coming?

OEDIPUS
  To tell him a small favor will gain him much.

STRANGER
  What service can a blind man render him?

OEDIPUS
  All I shall say will be clear-sighted indeed.

STRANGER
  Friend, listen to me: I wish you no injury;   75
  you seem wellborn, though obviously unlucky;
  stay where you are, exactly where I found you.
  And I'll inform the people of what you say—
  not in the town, but here—it rests with them
  to decide if you should stay or must move on.   80

                                        (Exit Stranger, to the side.)

OEDIPUS
  Child, has he gone?

ANTIGONE
  Yes, father. Now you may speak tranquilly,
  for only I am with you.

                    Ladies whose eyes
are terrible, Spirits, upon your sacred ground
I have first bent my knees in this new land;   85
therefore be mindful of me and of Apollo.
For when he gave me oracles of evil,
he also spoke of this: a resting place,
after long years, in the last country, where
I should find home among the sacred Furies: 90
that I might round out there my bitter life,
conferring benefit on those who received me,
a curse on those who have driven me away.
Portents, he said, would make me sure of this:
earthquake, thunder, or god's smiling lightning.°   95
But I am sure of it now, sure that you guided me
with feathery certainty° upon this road,
and led me here into your hallowed wood.
How otherwise could I, in my wandering,
have sat down first with you in all this land,
I who drink not, with you who love not wine?   100
How otherwise had I found this chair of stone?
Grant me then, goddesses, passage from life at last,
and consummation, as the unearthly voice foretold;°
unless indeed I seem not worth your grace,
slave as I am to such unending pain   105
as no man had before.
O hear my prayer,
sweet children of original Darkness! Hear me,
Athens, city named for great Athena,
honored above all cities in the world!
Pity a man's poor carcass and his ghost,
for Oedipus is not the strength he was.   110

ANTIGONE
   Be still. Some old, old men are coming this way,
   looking for the place where you are seated.

OEDIPUS

I shall be still. You get me clear of the path
and hide me in the wood, so I may hear
what they are saying. If we know their temper,   115
we shall be better able to act with prudence.

(Oedipus and Antigone move to one side, into the
grove. Enter the Chorus, from the other side.)

CHORUS [singing]

STROPHE A

Look for him. Who could he be? Where
is he? Where is the stranger
impious, blasphemous, shameless?   120
Use your eyes, search him out!
Cover the ground and uncover him!
Vagabond!
The old man must be a vagabond,
not of our land, for he'd never   125
otherwise dare to go in there,
in the inviolate thicket
of those whom it's futile to fight,°
those whom we tremble to name.
When we pass we avert our eyes—   130
            close our eyes!—
in silence, without conversation,
shaping our prayers with our lips.
But now, if the story is credible,
some alien fool has profaned it.
Yet I have looked over all the grove and   135
still cannot see him,
cannot say where he has hidden.

(Oedipus comes forward with Antigone.)

OEDIPUS [chanting in turn with the Chorus]

That stranger is I. As they say of the blind:
sounds are the things I see.

CHORUS
Ah!
His face is dreadful! His voice is dreadful!   140

OEDIPUS
I beg you not to think of me as a criminal.

CHORUS
Zeus defend us, who is this old man?

OEDIPUS
One whose fate is not quite to be envied.   145
O my masters, and men of this land;
that must be evident: why, otherwise,
should I need this girl
to lead me, her frailty to put my weight on?

CHORUS [*now singing*]
ANTISTROPHE A
Ah! His eyes are blind!   150
And were you brought into the world so?
Unhappy life—and so long!
Well, not if I can stop it
will you have this curse as well.
                    Stranger! You
trespass there! But beyond there,   155
in the glade where the grass is still,
where the honeyed libations drip
in the rill from the brimming spring,
you must not step. O stranger,   160
it is well to be careful about it!
Most careful!
Stand aside and come down then!
There is too much space between us!°
Say, wanderer, can you hear?   165
If you have a mind to tell us
your business, or wish to converse with our council,

come away from that place!
Only speak where it's proper to do so!

OEDIPUS [*chanting in turn with Antigone*]
    Now, daughter, what is the way of wisdom?   170

ANTIGONE
    We must do just as they do here, father;°
    we should give in now, and listen to them.

OEDIPUS
    Stretch out your hand to me.

ANTIGONE
                    There, I am with you.

OEDIPUS
    Sirs, let there be no injustice done me,
    once I have trusted you, and left my refuge.   175

                    (Led by Antigone, he moves forward.)

CHORUS [*singing in turn with Antigone and Oedipus*]
                    STROPHE B
    Never, never, will anyone drive you away
    from rest in this land, old man!

OEDIPUS
    Shall I come farther?

CHORUS
                    Yes, farther.

OEDIPUS
    And now?   180

CHORUS
                    You must guide him, girl;
    you can see how much further to come.

ANTIGONE
Come with your blind step, father;
this way; come where I lead you.

. . . .

CHORUS°
Stranger in a strange country,
courage, afflicted man!   185
Whatever the state abhors,
you too abhor, and honor
whatever the state holds dear.

OEDIPUS [chanting]
Lead me on, then, child,
to where we may speak or listen respectfully.   190
Let us not fight necessity.

CHORUS [singing]
                    ANTISTROPHE B
Now! Go no further than that platform there,
formed of the natural rock.

OEDIPUS
This?   195

CHORUS
              Far enough; you can hear us.

OEDIPUS
Shall I sit down?

CHORUS
              Yes, sit there to the side,
at the edge of the rock.

ANTIGONE
Father, this is where I can help you;
you must keep step with me; gently now.

OEDIPUS
Ah, me!

ANTIGONE

   Lean your old body on my arm;   200

   it is I, who love you; let yourself down.

OEDIPUS

   How bitter blindness is!

                          (He is seated on the rock, center.)

CHORUS

   Now that you are at rest, poor man,

   tell us, what is your name?

   Who are you, wanderer?   205

   What is the land of your ancestors?

OEDIPUS [*singing in turn with Antigone and the Chorus*]

                EPODE

   I am an exile, friends; but do not ask me . . .

CHORUS

   What is it you fear to say, old man?

OEDIPUS

   No, no, no! Do not go on

   questioning me! Do not ask my name!   210

CHORUS

   Why not?

OEDIPUS

                My star was unspeakable.°

CHORUS

                     Speak!

OEDIPUS

   My child, what can I say to them?

CHORUS

   Answer us, stranger: what is your family?   215

   Who was your father?

OEDIPUS

God help me, what will become of me, child?

ANTIGONE

Tell them; there is no other way.

OEDIPUS

Well, then, I will; I cannot hide it.

CHORUS

Between you, you greatly delay. Speak up!   220

OEDIPUS

Have you heard of Laius' family?

CHORUS

                              Ah!

OEDIPUS

Of the race of Labdacidae?

CHORUS

                         Ah, Zeus!

OEDIPUS

And ruined Oedipus?

CHORUS

                         You are he!

OEDIPUS

Do not take fright from what I say—

CHORUS

Oh, dreadful!

OEDIPUS

                    I am accursed.

CHORUS

                    Oh, fearful!

OEDIPUS

Antigone, what will happen now?   225

CHORUS

Away with you! Out with you! Leave our country!

OEDIPUS
And what of the promises you made me?

CHORUS
God will not punish the man
who makes return for an injury. 230
Deceivers may be deceived:
they play a game that ends
in grief, and not in pleasure.
Leave this grove at once!
Our country is not for you! 235
Wind no further
your clinging evil upon us!°

ANTIGONE [*still singing*]
O men of reverent mind!
Since you will not suffer my father,
old man though he is
and though you know his story—
he never knew what he did— 240
take pity still on my unhappiness;
and let me intercede with you for him.
Not with lost eyes, but looking in your eyes
as if I were a child of yours, I beg 245
mercy for him, the beaten man! O hear me!
We are thrown upon your mercy as on god's;
be kinder than you seem!°
By all you have and own that is dear to you,
children, wives, possessions, gods, I pray you! 250
For you will never see in all the world
a man whom god has led
escape his destiny!°

CHORUS LEADER [*now speaking*]
Child of Oedipus, indeed we pity you,
just as we pity him for his misfortune. 255
But we tremble to think of what the gods may do;
we dare not speak more generously!

OEDIPUS [*speaking*]

What use is reputation then? What good
comes of a noble name? A noble fiction!
For Athens, so they say, excels in piety;   260
has power to save the wretched of other lands,
can give them refuge, is unique in this.
Yet, when it comes to me, where is her refuge?
You pluck me from these rocks and cast me out,
all for fear of a name!   265
                    Or do you dread
my strength? my actions? I think not, for I
suffered those deeds more than I acted them,
as I might show if it were fitting here
to tell my father's and my mother's story . . .
for which you fear me, as I know too well.
And yet, how was I evil in myself?   270
I had been wronged, I retaliated; even had I
known what I was doing, was that evil?
Then, knowing nothing, I went on. Went on.
But those who wronged me knew, and ruined me.
Therefore I beg of you before the gods,   275
for the same cause that made you move me—
in reverence of your gods—give me this shelter,
and thus accord those powers what is theirs.
Think: their eyes are fixed upon the just,
fixed on the unjust too;° no impious man   280
can twist away from them forever.
Now, in their presence, do not blot your city's
luster by bending to unholy action.
As you would receive an honest petitioner,
give me, too, sanctuary; though my face   285
be dreadful in its look, yet honor me!
For I come here as one endowed with grace
by those who are over Nature; and I bring
advantage to this race, as you may learn

more fully when some lord of yours is here.° 290
Meanwhile be careful to be just.

CHORUS LEADER
          Old man.
This argument of yours compels our wonder.
It was not feebly worded. I am content
that higher authorities should judge this matter. 295

OEDIPUS
And where is he who rules the land, strangers?

CHORUS LEADER
In his father's city; but the messenger
who sent us here has gone to fetch him also.

OEDIPUS
Do you think a blind man will so interest him
as to bring him such a distance? 300

CHORUS LEADER
I do, indeed, when he has heard your name.

OEDIPUS
But who will tell him that?

CHORUS LEADER
It is a long road, and the rumors of travelers
have a way of wandering. He will have word of them.
Take heart—he will be here. Old man, your name 305
has gone over all the earth; though he may be
at rest when the news comes, he will come quickly.

OEDIPUS
Then may he come with luck for his own city
as well as for me. . . . The good befriend themselves.

ANTIGONE
O Zeus! What shall I say? How interpret this? 310

OEDIPUS
Antigone, my dear child, what is it?

ANTIGONE

           A woman
riding a Sicilian pony and coming toward us;
she is wearing the wide Thessalian sun hat.
I don't know!   315
Is it or isn't it? Or am I dreaming?
I think so; yes!—no. I can't be sure . . .
Ah, poor child,
it is no one else but she! And she is smiling   320
now as she comes! It is my dear Ismene!

OEDIPUS

What did you say, child?

                  (Ismene enters, with one attendant, from the side.)

ANTIGONE

            That I see your daughter!
My sister! Now you can tell her by her voice.

ISMENE

O father and sister together, dearest voices!°   325
Now I have found you—how, I scarcely know—
I don't know how I shall see you through my tears!

OEDIPUS

Child, have you come?

ISMENE

             Father, how old you seem!°

OEDIPUS

Child, are you here?

ISMENE

             And such a time I had!

OEDIPUS

Touch me, little one.

ISMENE

        I shall hold you both!

OEDIPUS

My children . . . and sisters.

ISMENE

        Oh, unhappy people!   330

OEDIPUS

She and I?

ISMENE

        And I with you, unhappy.

OEDIPUS

Why have you come, child?

ISMENE

        Thinking of you, father.

OEDIPUS

You were lonely?

ISMENE

        Yes; and I bring news for you.
I came with the one person I could trust.

OEDIPUS

Why, where are your brothers? Could they not do it?   335

ISMENE

They are—where they are. It is a hard time for them.

OEDIPUS

Ah! They behave as if they were Egyptians,
bred the Egyptian way! Down there, the men
sit indoors all day long, weaving;   340
the women go out and attend to business.
Just so your brothers, who should have done this work,
sit by the fire like home-loving girls,

and you two, in their place, must bear my hardships.   345
One, since her childhood ended and her body
gained its strength, has wandered ever with me,
an old man's governess; often in the wild
forest going without shoes, and hungry,
beaten by many rains, tired by the sun;   350
yet she rejected the sweet life of home
so that her father should have sustenance.
And you, my daughter, once before came out
unknown to Thebes, bringing me news of all
the oracle had said concerning me;   355
and you remained my faithful outpost there,
when I was driven from that land.
                              But now,
what news, Ismene, do you bring your father?
Why have you left your house to make this journey?
You came for no light reason, I know that;
it must be something serious for me.   360

ISMENE
I will pass over the troubles I have had
searching for your whereabouts, father.
They were hard enough to bear; and I will not
go through it all again in telling of them.
In any case, it is your sons' troubles   365
that I have come to tell you.
First it was their desire, as it was Creon's,
that the throne should pass to him; that thus the city
should be defiled no longer: such was their reasoning
when they considered our people's ancient curse
and how it enthralled your pitiful family.   370
But then some fury put it in their hearts—°
O pitiful again!—to itch for power,
for seizure of prerogative and throne.
And it was the younger and the less mature
who stripped his elder brother, Polynices,   375

[162] SOPHOCLES

of place and kingship, and then banished him.
But now the people hear he has gone to Argos,
into the valley land, has joined that nation,°
and is enlisting friends among its warriors:
telling them Argos shall honorably win   380
Thebes and her plain, or else eternal glory.°
This is not a mere recital, father,
but terrible truth!
How long will it be, I wonder,
before the gods take pity on your distress?

OEDIPUS
You have some hope then that they are concerned
with my deliverance?

ISMENE
                              I have, father.   385
The latest sentences of the oracle.

OEDIPUS
How are they worded? What do they prophesy?

ISMENE
That you shall be much solicited by our people
before your death—and after—for their welfare.   390

OEDIPUS
And what could anyone hope from such as I?

ISMENE
The oracles declare their strength's in you.

OEDIPUS
When I am worn to nothing, strength in me?

ISMENE
For the gods who threw you down sustain you now.

OEDIPUS
Slight favor, now I am old! My doom was early.   395

ISMENE

The proof of it is that Creon is coming to you
for that same reason, and soon: not by and by.

OEDIPUS

To do what, daughter? Tell me about this.

ISMENE

To settle you near the land of Thebes, and so
have you at hand; but you may not cross the border.   400

OEDIPUS

What good am I to Thebes outside the country?

ISMENE

It is merely that if your burial were unlucky
that would be perilous for them.

OEDIPUS

                              Ah, then!
This does not need divine interpretation.

ISMENE

Therefore they want to keep you somewhere near,
just at the border, where you'll not be free.   405

OEDIPUS

And will they compose my shade with Theban dust?°

ISMENE

Ah, father! No. Your father's blood forbids it.

OEDIPUS

Then they shall never hold me in their power!

ISMENE

If not, some day it will be bitter for them.

OEDIPUS

How will that be, my child?   410

ISMENE
When they shall stand
where you are buried, and feel your anger there.

OEDIPUS
What you have said—from whom did you hear it, child?

ISMENE
The envoys told me when they returned from Delphi.

OEDIPUS
Then all this about me was spoken there?

ISMENE
According to those men, just come to Thebes.   415

OEDIPUS
Has either of my sons had word of this?

ISMENE
They both have, and they understand it well.

OEDIPUS
The scoundrels! So they knew all this, and yet
would not give up the throne to have me back?

ISMENE
It hurts me to hear it, but I can't deny it.   420

OEDIPUS
Gods!
Never quench their fires of ambition!
Let the last word be mine upon this battle
they are about to join, with the spears lifting!
I'd see that he who holds the scepter now   425
will not have power long, nor would the other,
the banished one, return!
These were the two
who saw me in disgrace and banishment

and never lifted a hand for me. They heard me
howled from the country, heard the thing proclaimed!   430
And would you say I wanted exile then,
an appropriate clemency, granted by the state?
That is all false! The truth is that at first
my mind was a boiling caldron; nothing so sweet
as death, death by stoning, could have been given me;   435
yet no one there would grant me that desire.
It was only later, when my madness cooled,
and I had begun to think my rage excessive,
my punishment too great for what I had done;
then it was that the city—in its good time!—   440
decided to be harsh, and drove me out.
They could have helped me then; they could have
helped him who begot them! Would they do it?
For lack of a little word from that fine pair
out I went, a beggar, to wander forever!
Only by grace of these two girls, unaided,   445
have I got food or shelter or devotion;
their two brothers held their father of less worth
than sitting on a throne and being king.
Well, they shall never win me in their fight,°   450
nor will they profit from the rule of Thebes.
I am sure of that; I have heard the prophecies
brought by this girl; I think they fit those others
spoken so long ago, and now fulfilled.

   So let Creon be sent to find me: Creon,   455
or any other of influence in the state.
If you men here consent—as do those powers
holy and awful, the Spirits of this place—
to give me refuge, then shall this city have
a great savior, and woe to my enemies!   460

CHORUS LEADER
   Oedipus: you are surely worth our pity:
   you, and your children, too. And since you claim

also to be a savior of our land,
I'd like to give you counsel for good luck.

OEDIPUS

Dear friend! I'll do whatever you advise.   465

CHORUS LEADER

Make expiation to these divinities
whose ground you violated when you came.

OEDIPUS

In what way shall I do so? Tell me, friends.

CHORUS LEADER

First you must bring libations from the spring
that runs forever; and bring them with clean hands.   470

OEDIPUS

And when I have that holy water, then?

CHORUS LEADER

There are some bowls there, by a skillful potter;
put chaplets round the brims, over the handles.

OEDIPUS

Of myrtle sprigs, or woolen stuff, or what?

CHORUS LEADER

Take the fleeces cropped from a young lamb.   475

OEDIPUS

Just so; then how must I perform the rite?

CHORUS LEADER

Facing the quarter of the morning light
pour your libations out.

OEDIPUS

Am I to pour them from the bowls you speak of?

CHORUS LEADER

In three streams, yes; the last one, empty it.

OEDIPUS

With what should it be filled? Tell me this, too.   480

CHORUS LEADER

With water and honey; but with no wine added.

OEDIPUS

And when the leaf-dark earth receives it?

CHORUS LEADER

Lay three times nine young shoots of olive on it
with both your hands; meanwhile repeat this prayer:

OEDIPUS

This—I am eager to hear this, for it has great power.   485

CHORUS LEADER

That as we call them Eumenides,
which means the gentle of heart,
may they accept with gentleness
the suppliant and his wish.
So you, or he who prays for you, address them;
but do not speak aloud or raise a cry;
then come away, and do not turn again.   490
If you will do all this, I shall take heart
and stand up for you; otherwise, O stranger,
I should be seriously afraid for you.

OEDIPUS

Children, you hear the words of these good people?

ANTIGONE

Yes; now tell us what we ought to do.

OEDIPUS

It need not be performed by me; I'm far   495
from having the strength or sight for it—I have neither.
Let one of you go and carry out the ritual.
One soul, I think, often can make atonement
for many others, if it be devoted.

Now do it quickly—yet do not leave me alone!   500
I could not move without the help of someone.

ISMENE

I'll go and do it. But where am I to go?
Where shall I find the holy place, I wonder?

CHORUS LEADER

On the other side of the wood, girl. If you need it,
you may get help from the attendant there.

ISMENE

I am going now. Antigone, you will stay
and care for father. If it were difficult,
I should not think it so, since it is for him.°

(Exit Ismene to the side.)

CHORUS [*singing in turn with Oedipus*]
                        STROPHE A
What evil things have slept since long ago   510
it is not sweet to waken;
and yet I long to be told—

OEDIPUS

                What?

CHORUS

Of that heartbreak for which there was no help,
the pain you have had to suffer.

OEDIPUS

For kindness' sake, do not open   515
my old wound, and my shame.

CHORUS

It is told everywhere, and never dies;
I only want to hear it truly told.

OEDIPUS

Ah! Ah!

CHORUS
Consent I beg you!
Give me my wish, and I shall give you yours.   520

OEDIPUS
ANTISTROPHE A
I had to face a thing most terrible,
not willed by me, I swear;
I would have abhorred it all.

CHORUS
So?

OEDIPUS
Though I did not know, Thebes married me to evil;   525
Fate and I were joined there.

CHORUS
Then it was indeed your mother,
with whom the thing was done?°

OEDIPUS
Ah! It is worse than death to have to hear it!
Strangers! Yes: and these two girls of mine . . .   530

CHORUS
You say—

OEDIPUS
These luckless two
were given birth by her who gave birth to me.

CHORUS
STROPHE B
These then are daughters; they are also—

OEDIPUS
Sisters: yes, their father's sisters . . .   535

CHORUS
Ah, pity!

OEDIPUS
Pity, indeed. What throngs
of pities come into my mind!

CHORUS
You suffered—

OEDIPUS
Yes, unspeakably.

CHORUS
You sinned—

OEDIPUS
No, I did not sin!

CHORUS
How not?

OEDIPUS
I thought
of her as my reward. Ah, would that I had never won it!   540
Would that I had never served the state that day!°

CHORUS
ANTISTROPHE B
Unhappy man—and you also killed—

OEDIPUS
What is it now? What are you after?

CHORUS
Killed your father!

OEDIPUS
God in heaven!
You strike again where I am hurt.

CHORUS
You killed him.   545

OEDIPUS
Killed him. Yet, there is—

CHORUS
What more?

OEDIPUS
A just extenuation.
This:
I did not know him; and he wished to murder me.
Before the law—before god—I am innocent!°

(Enter Theseus from the side, with a retinue of soldiers.)

CHORUS LEADER
The king is coming! Aegeus' eldest son,
Theseus: news of you has brought him here.   550

THESEUS
In the old time I often heard men tell
of the bloody extinction of your eyes.
Even if on my way I were not informed,
I'd recognize you, son of Laius.
The garments and the tortured face   555
make plain your identity. I am sorry for you,
and I should like to know what favor here
you hope for from the city and from me:
both you and your unfortunate companion.
Tell me. It would be something dire indeed   560
to make me leave you comfortless; for I
too was an exile. I grew up abroad;
and in strange lands I fought as few men have
with danger and with death.
Therefore no wanderer shall come, as you do,   565
and be denied my audience or aid.
I know I am only a man; I have no more
to hope for in the end than you have.

OEDIPUS
Theseus, in those few words your nobility
is plain to me. I need not speak at length.   570

You have named me and my father accurately,
spoken with knowledge of my land and exile.
There is, then, nothing left for me to tell
but my desire; and then the tale is ended.

THESEUS

Tell me your wish, then; let me hear it now.   575

OEDIPUS

I come to give you something, and the gift
is my own beaten self: no feast for the eyes;
yet in me is a more lasting grace than beauty.

THESEUS

What grace is this you say you bring to us?°

OEDIPUS

In time you'll learn, but not immediately.   580

THESEUS

How long, then, must we wait to be enlightened?

OEDIPUS

Until I am dead, and you have buried me.

THESEUS

Your wish is burial? What of your life meanwhile?
Have you forgotten that?—or do you care?

OEDIPUS

It is all implicated in my burial.   585

THESEUS

But this is a brief favor you ask of me.

OEDIPUS

See to it, nevertheless! It is not simple.°

THESEUS

You mean I shall have trouble with your sons?

OEDIPUS

Those people want to take me back there now.

THESEUS

Will you not go? Is exile admirable?°   590

OEDIPUS

No. When I wished to go, they would not have it.

THESEUS

What childishness! You are surely in no position—

OEDIPUS

When you know me, admonish me; not now!

THESEUS

Instruct me then. I must not speak in ignorance.

OEDIPUS

Theseus, I have been wounded more than once.   595

THESEUS

Is it your family's curse that you refer to?

OEDIPUS

Not merely that; all Hellas talks of that.

THESEUS

Then what is the wound that is so pitiless?

OEDIPUS

Think how it is with me. I was expelled
from my own land by my own sons; and now,   600
as a parricide, my return is not allowed.

THESEUS

How can they summon you, if this is so?

OEDIPUS

The sacred oracle compels them to.

THESEUS

They fear some punishment from his forebodings?

OEDIPUS

They fear they will be struck down in this land! 605

THESEUS

And how could war arise between these nations?°

OEDIPUS

Most gentle son of Aegeus! The immortal
gods alone have neither age nor death!
All other things almighty Time disquiets. 610
Earth wastes away; the body wastes away;
faith dies; distrust is born;
and imperceptibly the spirit changes
between a man and his friend, or between two cities.
For some men soon, for others in later time,
their pleasure sickens; or love comes again. 615
And so with you and Thebes: the sweet season
holds between you now; but time goes on,
unmeasured Time, fathering numberless
nights, unnumbered days: and on one day
they'll break apart with spears this harmony—
all for a trivial word. 620
And then my sleeping and long-hidden corpse,
cold in the earth, will drink hot blood of theirs,
if Zeus endures; if his son's word is true.
    However: there's no felicity in speaking
of hidden things. Let me come back to this: 625
be careful that you keep your word to me;
for if you do you'll never say of Oedipus
that he was given refuge uselessly—
or if you say it, then the gods have lied.

CHORUS LEADER

My lord: before you came this man gave promise
of having power to make his words come true. 630

THESEUS

Who would reject his friendship? Is he not

one who would have, in any case, an ally's
right to our hospitality?
Moreover he has asked grace of our deities,
and offers no small favor in return.   635
As I value that favor, I shall not refuse
this man's desire; I declare him a citizen.
And if it should please our friend to remain here,
I direct you to take care of him;
or else he may come with me.
                     Whatever you choose,   640
Oedipus, we shall be happy to accord.
You know your own needs best; I accede to them.

OEDIPUS

May god bless men like these!

THESEUS

What do you say then? Shall it be my house?

OEDIPUS

If it were right for me. But the place is here . . .

THESEUS

And what will you do here?—not that I oppose you.   645

OEDIPUS

Here I shall prevail over those who banished me.

THESEUS

Your presence, as you say, is a great blessing.

OEDIPUS

If you are firm in doing what you promise.

THESEUS

You can be sure of me; I'll not betray you.

OEDIPUS

I'll not ask pledges, as I would of scoundrels.   650

THESEUS

You'd get no more assurance than by my word.

OEDIPUS

I wonder how you will behave?

THESEUS

You fear?

OEDIPUS

That men will come—

THESEUS

These men will attend to them.

OEDIPUS

Look: when you leave me—

THESEUS

I know what to do!

OEDIPUS

I am oppressed by fear!

THESEUS

I feel no fear.   655

OEDIPUS

You do not know the menace!

THESEUS

I do know
no man is going to take you against my will.
Angry men are liberal with threats°
and bluster generally. When the mind
is master of itself, threats are no matter.   660
These people may have dared to talk quite fiercely
of taking you; perhaps, as I rather think,
they'll find a sea of troubles in the way.
Therefore I should advise you to take heart.

Even aside from me and my intentions,
did not Apollo send and guide you here?   665
However it may be, I can assure you,
while I'm away, my name will be your shield.

> *(Exit Theseus and soldiers, to the side.)*

CHORUS [*singing*]

STROPHE A

The land of running horses, fair
Colonus takes a guest;   670
he shall not seek another home.°
For this, in all the earth and air,
is most secure and loveliest.

In the god's untrodden vale
where leaves and berries throng,
and wine-dark ivy climbs the bough,
the sweet, sojourning nightingale   675
murmurs all night long.

No sun nor wind may enter there
nor the winter's rain;
but ever through the shadow goes
Dionysus reveler,
immortal maenads in his train.   680

ANTISTROPHE A

Here with drops of heaven's dews
at daybreak all the year,
the clusters of narcissus bloom,
time-hallowed garlands for the brows
of those great Ladies whom we fear.

The crocus like a little sun
blooms with its yellow ray;   685
the river's fountains are awake,
and his nomadic streams that run
unthinned forever, and never stay,°

But like perpetual lovers move
on the maternal land.   690
And here the choiring Muses come,
and the divinity of Love,
with the gold reins in her hand.

STROPHE B

And our land has a thing unknown
on Asia's sounding coast   695
or in the sea-surrounded west
where Pelops' kin holds sway:°
the olive, fertile and self-sown,
the terror of our enemies
that no hand tames nor tears away—
the blessed tree that never dies!—   700
but it will mock the spearsman in his rage.

Ah, how it flourishes in every field,
most beautifully here!
The gray-leafed tree, the children's nourisher!
No young man nor one partnered by his age
knows how to root it out nor make
barren its yield;
for Zeus Protector of the Shoot has sage   705
eyes that forever are awake,
and Pallas watches with her sea-gray eyes.

ANTISTROPHE B

Last and grandest praise I sing
to Athens, nurse of men,
for her great pride and for the splendor   710
destiny has conferred on her.
Land from which fine horses spring!
Land where foals are beautiful!
Land of the sea and the seafarer,
enthroned on her pure littoral
by Cronus' briny son in ancient time.

That lord, Poseidon, must I praise again
who found our horsemen fit   715
for first bestowal of the curb and bit,
to discipline the stallion in his prime;
and strokes to which our oarsmen sing,
well-fitted, oak and men,
whose long sea-oars in wondrous rhyme
flash from the salt foam, following
the track of winds on waters virginal.°

ANTIGONE
Land so well spoken of and praised so much!   720
Now is the time to show those words are true.

OEDIPUS
What now, my child?

ANTIGONE
                    A man is coming toward us,
and it is Creon—not alone, though, father.

OEDIPUS
Most kindly friends! I hope you may give proof,
and soon, of your ability to protect me!   725

CHORUS LEADER
No fear: it will be proved. I may be old,
but the nation's strength has not grown old.

                    (Enter Creon from the side, with soldiers.)

CREON
Gentlemen, and citizens of this land:
I can see from your eyes that my arrival
has been a cause of sudden fear to you.   730
Do not be fearful; and say nothing hostile!
I have not come for any hostile action:
for I am old, and know this city has
power, if any city in Hellas has.

But for this man here: I, despite my age,   735
am sent to bring him to the land of Thebes.°
This is not one man's mission, but was ordered
by the whole Theban people. I am their emissary,
because it fell to me as a relative
to mourn his troubles more than anyone.
　　　So, now, poor Oedipus, come home.   740
You know the word I bring. Your countrymen
are right in summoning you—I most of all,
for most of all, unless I am worst of men,
I grieve for your unhappiness, old man.
I see you ravaged as you are, a stranger   745
everywhere, never at rest,
with only a girl to serve you in your need—
I never thought she'd fall to such indignity,
poor child! And yet she has,
forever tending you, leading a beggar's   750
life with you; a grown-up girl who knows
nothing of marriage; whoever comes can take her . . .
　　　Is not this a disgrace? I weep to see it!
Disgrace for you, for me, for all our people!
We cannot hide what is so palpable.   755
But you, if you will listen to me, Oedipus—
and in the name of your father's gods, listen!—
bury the whole thing now;° agree with me
to go back to your city and your home!
Take friendly leave of Athens, as she merits;
but you should have more reverence for Thebes,
since long ago she was your kindly nurse.   760

OEDIPUS

You brazen rascal! Playing your rascal's tricks
in righteous speeches, as you always would!
Why do you try it? How can you think to take me
into that snare I should so hate if taken?
That time when I was sick with my own life's   765

evil, when I would gladly have left my land,
you had no mind to give me what I wanted!
But when at long last I had had my fill
of rage and grief, and in my quiet house
began to find some comfort: that was the time
you chose to rout me out. 770
How precious was this kinship to you then?
It is the same thing now: you see this city
and all its people being kind to me,
so you would draw me away—
a cruel thing, for all your soothing words.
Why is it your pleasure to be amiable 775
to those who do not want your amiability?
Suppose that when you begged for something desperately
a man should neither grant it you nor give
sympathy even; but later when you were glutted
with all your heart's desire, should give it then,
when charity was no charity at all?
Would you not think the kindness somewhat hollow? 780
That is the sort of kindness you offer me:
generous in words, but in reality evil.
Now I will tell these men, and prove you evil.
You come to take me, but not to take me home;
rather to settle me outside the city 785
so that the city may escape my curse,
escape from punishment by Athens.
                              Yes;
but you'll not have it. What you'll have is this:
my vengeance active in that land forever.
And what my sons will have of my old kingdom
is just so much room as they need to die in! 790
        Now who knows better the destiny of Thebes?
I do, for I have had the best informants:
Apollo, and Zeus himself who is his father.
And yet you come here with your fraudulent speech

all whetted up! The more you talk, the more   795
harm, not good, you'll get by it!—
however, I know you'll never believe that—
only leave us! Let us live here in peace!
Is this misfortune, if it brings contentment?

CREON

Which of us do you consider is more injured   800
by talk like this? You hurt only yourself.

OEDIPUS

I am perfectly content, so long as you
can neither wheedle me nor fool these others.

CREON

Unhappy man! Shall it be plain that time
brings you no wisdom? that you shame your age?   805

OEDIPUS

An agile wit! I know no honest man
able to speak so well under all conditions!

CREON

To speak much is one thing; to speak to the point's another!

OEDIPUS

As if you spoke so little but so fittingly!

CREON

No, not fittingly for a mind like yours!   810

OEDIPUS

Leave me! I speak for these men, too!
Spare me your wardship, here where I must live!

CREON

I call on these—not you!—as witnesses
of what rejoinder you have made to friends.
If I ever take you—

OEDIPUS
    With these men opposing,
    who is going to take me by violence?   815

CREON
    You'll suffer without need of that, I promise you!

OEDIPUS
    What are you up to? What is behind that brag?

CREON
    Your daughters: one of them I have just now
    had seized and carried off; now I'll take this one!

OEDIPUS
    Ah!

CREON
                    Soon you shall have more reason to groan about it!   820

OEDIPUS
    You have my child?

CREON
                    And this one in a moment!

OEDIPUS
    Ah, friends! What will you do? Will you betray me?
    Expel this man who has profaned your country!

CHORUS LEADER
    Go, and go quickly, stranger! You have no right
    to do what you are doing, or what you have done!   825

CREON   (To his soldiers.)
    You there: it would be well to take her now,
    whether she wants to go with you or not.

                            (Two soldiers approach Antigone.)

ANTIGONE
    Oh, god, where shall I run? What help is there
    From gods or men?

CHORUS LEADER
What are you doing, stranger?

CREON
I will not touch this man; but she is mine.   830

OEDIPUS
O masters of this land!

CHORUS LEADER
This is unjust!

CREON
No, just!

CHORUS LEADER
Why so?

CREON
I take what belongs to me!

OEDIPUS [*now singing*]

STROPHE

O Athens!

(The soldiers seize Antigone.)

CHORUS [*mostly singing while Creon, Antigone, and Oedipus speak in response*]
What are you doing, stranger? Will you   835
Let her go? Must we have a test of strength?

CREON
Hold off!

CHORUS
Not while you persist in doing this!

CREON
Your city will have war if you hurt me!

OEDIPUS
Did I not foretell this?

CHORUS LEADER

        Take your hands
off the child at once!

CREON

        What you cannot enforce,
do not command!

CHORUS LEADER

  Release the child, I say!

CREON

        And I say—march!   840

CHORUS

  Help! Here, men of Colonus! Help! Help!
  The city, my city, is violated!
  Help, ho!

ANTIGONE

  They drag me away. How wretched! O friends, friends!

OEDIPUS

  Where are you, child?

ANTIGONE

        They have overpowered me!   845

OEDIPUS

  Give me your hands, little one!

ANTIGONE

        I cannot do it!

CREON   *(To the soldiers.)*

  Will you get on with her?

        (Exit the guards to one side, dragging Antigone.)

OEDIPUS

        God help me now!°

CREON

    With these two sticks at any rate you'll never
guide yourself again. But since you wish
to conquer your own people—by whose command,   850
though I am royal, I have performed this act—
go on and conquer! Later, I think, you'll learn
that now as before you have done yourself no good
by gratifying your temper against your friends!
Anger has always been your greatest sin!   855

CHORUS LEADER   *(To Creon, approaching him.)*

    Control yourself, stranger!

CREON

             Don't touch me, I say!

CHORUS LEADER

    I'll not release you! Those two girls were stolen!

CREON

    By god, I'll have more plunder in a moment
to bring my city! I'll not stop with them!

CHORUS LEADER

    Now what are you about?   860

CREON

             I'll take him, too!

CHORUS LEADER

    A terrible thing to say!

CREON

             It will be done!

CHORUS LEADER

    Not if the ruler of our land can help it!°

OEDIPUS

    Voice of shamelessness! Will you touch me?

CREON

    Silence, I say!

OEDIPUS

             No! May the powers here
not make me silent until I say this curse: 865
you scoundrel, who have cruelly taken her
who served my naked eyepits as their eyes!
On you and yours forever may the sun god,
watcher of all the world, confer such days
as I have had, and such an age as mine!   870

CREON

    Do you see this, men of the land of Athens?

OEDIPUS

    They see both me and you; and they see also
that when I am hurt I have only words to avenge it!

CREON

    I'll not stand for it longer! Alone as I am,
and slow with age, I'll try my strength to take him!   875

                    (Creon advances toward Oedipus.)

OEDIPUS
               ANTISTROPHE

    Ah!

CHORUS

    You are a bold man, friend,
    if you think you can do this!

CREON

    I do think so!

CHORUS

    If you could, our city would be finished!   880

CREON

    In a just cause the weak will beat the strong!

OEDIPUS

    You hear his talk?

CHORUS LEADER

            By Zeus, he shall not do it!°

CREON

    Zeus may determine that, but you will not.

CHORUS LEADER

    Is this not criminal?

CREON   *(Laying hold of Oedipus.)*

            If so, you'll bear it!

CHORUS [*singing*]

    Ho, everyone! Captains, ho!
    Come on the run!   885
    They are well on their way by now!

            (Enter Theseus from the side, with armed men.)

THESEUS

    Why do you shout? What is the matter here?
    Of what are you afraid?
    You have interrupted me as I was sacrificing
    to the great sea god, the patron of Colonus.
    Tell me, let me know everything;
    I do not care to make such haste for nothing.   890

OEDIPUS

    O dearest friend—I recognize your voice—
    a fearful thing has just been done to me!

THESEUS

    What is it? Who is the man who did it? Tell me.

OEDIPUS

    This Creon has had my daughters bound and stolen.   895

THESEUS

    What's this you say?

OEDIPUS

Yes; now you know my loss.

THESEUS   *(To his men.)*

One of you go on the double
to the altar place and rouse the people there;
make them leave the sacrifice at once
and run full speed, both foot and cavalry
as hard as they can gallop, for the place   900
where the two highways come together.
The girls must not be taken past that point,
or I shall be a laughingstock to this fellow,
as if I were a man to be handled roughly!
Go on, do as I tell you! Quick!

(Exit a soldier, to the side.)

This man—

if I should act in anger, as he deserves,   905
I would not let him leave my hands unbloodied;
but he shall be subject to the sort of laws
he has himself imported here.—

(To Creon.)

You: you shall never leave this land of Attica
until you produce those girls here in my presence;   910
for your behavior is an affront to me,
a shame to your own people and your nation.
You come to a city-state that practices justice,
a state that rules by law, and by law only;
and yet you cast aside her authority,   915
take what you please, and worse, by violence,
as if you thought there were no men among us,
or only slaves; and as if I were nobody.

I doubt that Thebes is responsible for you:
she has no propensity for breeding rascals.   920
And Thebes would not applaud you if she knew
you tried to trick me and to rob the gods

by dragging helpless people from their sanctuary!
Were I a visitor in your country—
no matter how immaculate my claims—   925
without consent from him who ruled the land,
whoever he might be, I'd take nothing.
I think I have some notion of the conduct
proper to one who visits a friendly city.
You bring disgrace upon an honorable
land—your own land, too; a long life   930
seems to have left you witless as you are old.
        I said it once and say it now again:
someone had better bring those girls here quickly,
unless you wish to prolong your stay with us
under close guard, and not much liking it.   935
This is not just a speech; I mean it, friend.

CHORUS LEADER

Now do you see where you stand? Thebes is just;
but you are adjudged to have acted wickedly.

CREON

It was not that I thought this state unmanly,
son of Aegeus; nor ill-governed, either;   940
rather I did this thing in the opinion
that no one here would love my citizens°
so tenderly as to keep them against my will . . .
And surely, I thought, no one would give welcome
to an unholy man, a parricide,
a man with whom his mother had been found!°   945
Such at least was my estimate of the wisdom
native to the Areopagus; I thought
Athens was not a home for such exiles.
In that belief I considered him my prize.   950
Even so, I'd not have touched him had he not
called down curses on my race and me;
that was an injury that deserved reprisal.
There is no old age for a man's anger.

Only death; the dead cannot be hurt.° 955
    You will do as you wish in this affair,
for even though my case is right and just,
I am weak, without support. Nevertheless,
old as I am, I'll try to hold you answerable.

OEDIPUS

O arrogance unashamed! Whose age do you 960
think you are insulting, mine or yours?
The bloody deaths, the incest, the calamities
you speak so glibly of: I suffered them
by fate, against my will! It was god's pleasure,
and perhaps our family had angered him long ago.° 965
In me myself you could not find such evil
as would have made me sin against my own.
And tell me this: if there were prophecies
repeated by the oracles of the gods,
that father's death should come through his own son, 970
how could you justly blame it upon me?
On me, who was yet unborn, yet unconceived,
not yet existent for my father and mother?
If then I came into the world—as I did come—
in wretchedness, and met my father in fight
and knocked him down, not knowing that I killed him 975
nor whom I killed°—again, how could you find
guilt in that unmeditated act?
As for my mother—damn you, you have no shame,
though you are her own brother, in forcing me
to speak of that unspeakable marriage;
but I shall speak, I'll not be silent now 980
after you've let your foul talk go so far!
Yes, she gave me birth—incredible fate!—
but neither of us knew the truth; and she
bore my children also—and then her shame.
But one thing I do know: you are content 985
to slander her as well as me for that;

while I would not have married her willingly
nor willingly would I ever speak of it.
No: I shall not be judged an evil man,
neither in that marriage nor in that death
which you forever charge me with so bitterly.   990
      Just answer me one thing:
if someone tried to kill you here and now,
you righteous gentleman, what would you do,
inquire first if the stranger was your father?
Or would you not first try to defend yourself?
I think that since you like to be alive   995
you'd treat him as the threat required; not
look around for assurance that you were right.
Well, that was the sort of danger I was in,
forced into it by the gods. My father's soul,
were it on earth, I know would bear me out.
You, however—being a knave, and since you   1000
think it fair to say anything you choose
and speak of what should not be spoken of—
accuse me of all this before these people.
      You also think it clever to flatter Theseus,
and Athens—her exemplary government.
But in your flattery you have forgotten this: 1005
if any country comprehends the honors
due to the gods, this country knows them best.
Yet you would steal me from Athens in my age
and in my time of prayer;° indeed, you seized me
and you have seized and carried off my daughters.
      Now for that profanation I make my prayer,   1010
calling on the divinities of the grove
that they shall give me aid and fight for me,
so you may know what men defend this town.

CHORUS LEADER
   My lord, our friend is worthy; he has had
   disastrous fortune; yet he deserves our comfort.   1015

THESEUS

    Enough of speeches. While the perpetrators
    flee, we who were injured loiter here.

CREON

    What will you have me do?—since I am worthless.

THESEUS

    You lead us on the way. You can be my escort.
    If you are holding the children in this neighborhood,   1020
    you yourself will uncover them to me.
    If your retainers have taken them in flight,
    the chase is not ours; others are after them,
    and they will never have cause to thank their gods
    for getting free out of this country.
    All right. Move on. And remember that the captor   1025
    is now the captive; the hunter is in the snare.
    What was won by stealth will not be kept.
    In this you'll not have others to assist you;
    and I know well you had them, for you'd never
    dare to go so far in your insolence   1030
    were you without sufficient accomplices.
    You must have had a reason for your confidence,
    and I must reckon with it. The whole city
    must not seem overpowered by one man.°
    Do you understand at all? Or do you think
    that what I say is still without importance?   1035

CREON

    To what you say I make no objection here.
    At home we, too, shall determine what to do.

THESEUS

    If you must threaten, do so on the way.
    Oedipus, you stay here, and rest assured
    that unless I perish first I'll not draw breath   1040
    until I put your children in your hands.

OEDIPUS

    Bless you for your noble heart, Theseus,
    and you are blessed in what you do for us.°

                (Exit Theseus and Creon to the side, with the soldiers.)

CHORUS [*singing*]

STROPHE A

Ah, god, to be where the pillagers make stand!°
To hear the shout and brazen sound of war!   1045
Or maybe on Apollo's sacred strand,
or by that torchlit Eleusinian shore

Where pilgrims come, whose lips the golden key   1050
of sweet-voiced Ministers has rendered still.
To cherish there with grave Persephone
consummate rest from death and mortal ill;

For even to those shades the warrior king   1055
will press the fighting on—until he take
the virgin sisters from the foemen's ring,
within his country, for his country's sake!

ANTISTROPHE A

It may be they will get beyond the plain
and reach the snowy mountain's western side.   1060
If their light chariots have the racing rein,
if they have ponies, and if they can ride;

Yet they'll be taken: for the god they fear
fights for our land, and Theseus sends forth   1065
his breakneck cavalry with all its gear
flashing like mountain lightning to the north.

These are the riders of Athens, conquered never;°
they honor her whose glory all men know,
and honor the sea god, who is dear forever   1070
to Rhea Mother, who bore him long ago.

Swords out—or has the work of swords begun?
My mind leans to a whisper: 1075
within the hour they must surrender
the woeful children of the blinded one;
this day is shaped by Zeus Artificer.
I can call up the bright sword play,°   1080
but wish the wind would lift me like a dove
under the tall cloud cover
to look with my own eyes on this affray.

Zeus, lord of all, and eye of heaven on all,   1085
let our home troop's hard riding
cut them off, and a charge from hiding
carry the combat in one shock and fall.
Stand, helmeted Athena, at our side,   1090
Apollo, Artemis, come down,
hunter and huntress of the flickering deer—
pace with each cavalier
for honor of our land and Athens town.°   1095

CHORUS LEADER [*speaking*]
    O wanderer! You will not say I lied;
    I who kept lookout for you!
    I see them now—the two girls—here they come
    with our armed men around them.

OEDIPUS
    What did you say? Ah, where?

> (*Enter Theseus from the side, leading Antigone*
> *and Ismene, escorted by soldiers.*)

ANTIGONE
                    Father, father!
    I wish some god would give you eyes to see   1100
    the noble prince who brings us back to you!

OEDIPUS
Ah, child! You are really here?

ANTIGONE
                          Yes, for the might
of Theseus and his kind followers saved us.

OEDIPUS
Come to your father, child, and let me touch you both,
whom I had thought never to touch again!   1105

ANTIGONE
It shall be as you ask; I wish it as much as you.

OEDIPUS
Where are you?

ANTIGONE
                          We are coming to you together.

OEDIPUS
My sweet children!

ANTIGONE
                          To our father, sweet indeed.

OEDIPUS
My staff and my support!

ANTIGONE
                          And partners in sorrow.

OEDIPUS
I have what is dearest to me in the world: 1110
to die, now, would not be so terrible
since you are near me.
                          Press close to me, child,
be rooted in your father's arms; rest now
from the cruel separation, the going and coming;
and tell me the story as briefly as you can: 1115
a little talk is enough for girls so tired.°

ANTIGONE

Theseus saved us: he is the one to tell you,
and he can put it briefly and make it clear.°

OEDIPUS

Dear friend: don't be offended if I continue
to talk to these two children overlong;   1120
I had scarce thought they would be seen again!
Be sure I understand that you alone
made this joy possible for me.
You are the one that saved them, no one else,
and may the gods give you such destiny
as I desire for you and for your country.   1125
For I have found you truly reverent,
decent, and straight in speech, you only
of all mankind.
I know it, and I thank you with these words.
All that I have I owe to your courtesy.
Now give me your right hand, my lord,   1130
and if it be permitted, let me kiss you . . .
        What am I saying? How can a wretch like me
desire to touch a man who has no stain
of evil in him? No, no; I will not do it;
and neither shall you touch me. The only ones
fit to be fellow sufferers of mine   1135
are those with such experience as I have.
Receive my salutation where you are;
and for the rest, be kindly to me still
as you have been up to now.

THESEUS

That you should talk a long time to your children
in joy at seeing them—why, that's no wonder!   1140
Or that you should address them before me—
there's no offense in that. It is not in words
that I should wish my life to be distinguished,
but rather in things done.

Have I not shown that? I was not a liar   1145
in what I swore I'd do for you, old man.
I am here; and I have brought them back
alive and safe, for all they were threatened with.
As to how I found them, how I took them, why
brag of it? You will surely learn from them.
However, there is a matter that just now   1150
came to my attention on my way here—
a trivial thing to speak of, and yet puzzling;
I want your opinion on it.
It is best for a man not to neglect such things.

OEDIPUS

What is it, son of Aegeus? Tell me,
so I may know on what you desire counsel.   1155

THESEUS

They say a man is here claiming to be
a relative of yours, though not of Thebes;
for some reason he has thrown himself in prayer°
before Poseidon's altar, where I was making
sacrifice before I came.

OEDIPUS

What is his country? What is he praying for?   1160

THESEUS

All I know is this: he asks, they tell me,
a brief interview with you, and nothing more.

OEDIPUS

Upon what subject?
If he's in prayer, it cannot be a trifle.

THESEUS

They say he only asks to speak to you
and then to depart safely by the same road.   1165

OEDIPUS

Who could it be that would come here to pray?°

THESEUS
    Think: have you any relative in Argos
    who might desire this favor of you?

OEDIPUS
                    Dear friend!
    Say no more!

THESEUS
                    What has alarmed you?

OEDIPUS
    No more!

THESEUS
                    But what is the matter? Tell me.   1170

OEDIPUS
    When I heard "Argos" I knew the petitioner.

THESEUS
    And who is he whom I must hold at fault?

OEDIPUS
    A son of mine, my lord, and a hated one:
    nothing could be more painful than to listen to him.

THESEUS
    But why? Is it not possible to listen   1175
    without doing anything you need not do?
    Why should it distress you so to hear him?

OEDIPUS
    My lord, even his voice is hateful to me.
    Don't overrule me; don't make me yield in this!

THESEUS
    But now consider if you are not obliged
    to do so by his supplication here:
    perhaps you have a duty to the god.   1180

ANTIGONE

Father, listen to me, even if I am young.
Allow this man to satisfy his conscience
and give the gods whatever he thinks their due.
And let our brother come here, for our sake.
Don't be afraid: he will not throw you off   1185
in your resolve, nor speak offensively.
What is the harm in hearing what he says?
If he has ill intentions, he'll betray them.
You sired him; even though he wrongs you, father,
and wrongs you impiously, still you cannot   1190
rightfully wrong him in return!
Do let him come!
                    Other men have bad sons,
and other men are swift to anger; yet
they will accept advice, they will be swayed
by their friends' pleading, even against their nature.
Reflect, not on the present, but on the past;   1195
think of your mother's and your father's fate
and what you suffered through them! If you do,
I think you'll see how terrible an end
terrible wrath may have.
You have, I think, a permanent reminder
in your lost, irrecoverable eyes.   1200
Ah, yield to us! If our request is just,
we need not, surely, be importunate;
and you, to whom I have not yet been hard,
should not be obdurate with me!°

OEDIPUS

Child, your talk wins you a pleasure
that will be pain for me. If you have set   1205
your heart on it, so be it.
Only, Theseus: if he is to come here,
let no one have power over my life!

THESEUS

That is the sort of thing I need hear only
once, not twice, old man. I do not boast,
but you should know, your life is safe while mine is.° 1210

(Exit Theseus to the side, with his soldiers, leaving two on guard.)

CHORUS [singing]

STROPHE

Though he has watched a decent age pass by,
a man will sometimes still desire the world.
I swear I see no wisdom in that man.
The endless hours pile up a drift of pain
more unrelieved each day; and as for pleasure,
when he is sunken in excessive age 1215
you will not see his pleasure anywhere.
The last attendant is the same for all,
old men and young alike, as in its season 1220
man's heritage of underworld appears:
there being then no epithalamion,
no music and no dance. Death is the finish.

ANTISTROPHE

Not to be born surpasses thought and speech.
The second best is to have seen the light 1225
and then to go back quickly whence we came.
The feathery follies of his youth once over,
what trouble is beyond the range of man? 1230
What heavy burden will he not endure?
Jealousy, faction, quarreling, and battle—
the bloodiness of war, the grief of war. 1235
And in the end he comes to strengthless age,
abhorred by all men, without company,
unfriended in that uttermost twilight
where he must live with every bitter thing.

EPODE

This is the truth, not for me only,

but for this blind and ruined man.   1240
Think of some shore in the north,
the concussive waves make stream
this way and that in the gales of winter:
it is like that with him,
the wild wrack breaking over him
from head to foot, and coming on forever;   1245
now from the plunging down of the sun,
now from the sunrise quarter,
now from where the noonday gleams,
now from the night and the north.

ANTIGONE

I think I see the stranger near us now,
and no men with him, father; but his eyes   1250
swollen with weeping as he comes.

                                        (Enter Polynices, from the side.)

OEDIPUS
                    Who comes?

ANTIGONE

The one whom we have had so long in mind;
it is he who stands here; it is Polynices.

POLYNICES

Ah, now what shall I do? Sisters, shall I
weep for my misfortunes or for those   1255
I see in the old man, my father,
whom I have found here in an alien land,
with two frail girls, an outcast for so long,
and with such garments! The abominable
filth grown old with him, rotting his sides!   1260
And on his sightless face the ragged hair
streams in the wind. There's the same quality
in the food he carries for his thin old belly.
All this I learn too late.

And I swear now that I have been villainous   1265
in not supporting you! You need not wait
to hear it said by others!
                    Only, think:
compassion limits even the power of god;°
so may there be a limit with you, father!
For all that has gone wrong may still be healed,   1270
and surely the worst is passed!
Why are you silent?
Speak to me, father! Don't turn away from me!
Will you not answer me at all? Will you
send me away without a word?
                    Not even
tell me why you are enraged against me?
Daughters of Oedipus, my own sisters,   1275
try to move your so implacable father;
do not let him reject me in such contempt!
Make him reply! I am here on pilgrimage . . .°

ANTIGONE

Poor brother: you yourself must tell him why.   1280
As men speak on they may sometimes give pleasure,
sometimes annoy, or sometimes touch the heart;
and so somehow provide the mute with voices.

POLYNICES

I will speak out then; your advice is fair.
First, however, I must claim the help   1285
of that same god, Poseidon, from whose altar
the governor of this land has lifted me
and sent me here, giving me leave to speak
and to await response, and a safe passage.
These are the favors I desire from you,
strangers, and from my sisters and my father.   1290
        And now, father, I will tell you why I came.
I am a fugitive, driven from my country,

because I thought fit, as the eldest born,
to take my seat upon your sovereign throne.
For that, Eteocles, the younger of us, 1295
banished me—but not by a decision
in argument or ability or arms;
merely because he won the city over.
Of this I believe the Furies that pursue you
were indeed the cause: and so I hear
from clairvoyants whom I afterward consulted . . .° 1300
Then, when I went to the Dorian land of Argos,
I took Adrastus as my father-in-law,
and bound to me by oath whatever men
were known as leaders or as fighters there;
my purpose being to form an expedition
of seven troops of spearmen against Thebes, 1305
with which enlistment may I die for justice
or else expel the men who exiled me!
     So it is. Then why should I come here now?
Father, my prayers must be made to you,
mine and those of all who fight with me. 1310
Their seven columns under seven captains
even now complete the encirclement of Thebes:
men like Amphiaraus, the hard spear-thrower,
expert in spears and in the ways of eagles;
second is Tydeus, the Aetolian, 1315
son of Oeneus; third is Eteoclus,
born in Argos; fourth is Hippomedon
(his father, Talaus, sent him); Capaneus,
the fifth, has sworn he'll raze the town of Thebes
with fire-brands; and sixth is Parthenopaeus,
an Arcadian who roused himself to war— 1320
son of that virgin famous in the old time
who long years afterward conceived and bore him—
Parthenopaeus, Atalanta's son.
And it is I, your son—or if I am not

truly your son, since evil fathered me,
at least I am called your son—it is I who lead
the fearless troops of Argos against Thebes.   1325
      Now in the name of these two children, father,
and for your own soul's sake, we all implore
and beg you to give up your heavy wrath
against me! I go forth to punish him,
the brother who robbed me of my fatherland.   1330
If we can put any trust in oracles,
they say that those you bless shall come to power.
Now by the gods and fountains of our people,
I pray you, listen and comply! Are we not beggars
both of us, and exiles, you and I?   1335
We live by paying court to other men;
the same fate follows us.
But as for him—how insupportable!—
he lords it in our house, luxuriates there,
laughs at us both!
If you will stand by me in my resolve,   1340
I'll waste no time or trouble whipping him;°
and then I'll reestablish you at home,
and settle there myself, and throw him out.
If your will is the same as mine, it's possible
to promise this. If not, I can't be saved.   1345

CHORUS LEADER
  For the sake of the one who sent him, Oedipus,
  speak to this man before you send him back.

OEDIPUS
  Yes, gentlemen: but were it not Theseus,
  the sovereign of your land, who sent him here,
  thinking it right that he should have an answer,   1350
  you never would have heard a sound from me.
  Well: he has asked, and he shall hear from me
  a kind of answer that will not overjoy him.
  You scoundrel! When it was you who held

throne and authority—as your brother now
holds them in Thebes—you drove me into exile: 1355
me, your own father: made me a homeless man,
insuring me these rags you maunder over°
when you behold them—now that you, as well,
have fallen on evil days and are in exile.
Weeping is no good now. However long   1360
my life may last, I have to see it through;
but I regard you as a murderer!
For you reduced me to this misery;
you made me an exile; because of you
I have begged my daily bread from other men.
If I had not these daughters to sustain me,   1365
I might have lived or died for all your interest.
But they have saved me; they are my support,
and are not girls, but men, in faithfulness.
As for you two, you are no sons of mine!

    And so it is that there are eyes that watch you°   1370
even now; though not as they shall watch
if those troops are in fact marching on Thebes.
You cannot take that city. You'll go down
all bloody,° and your brother, too. For I
have placed that curse upon you before this,   1375
and now I invoke that curse to fight for me,
that you may see a reason to respect
your parents, though your birth was as it was;
and though I am blind, not to dishonor me.
These girls did not.
And so your supplication and your throne   1380
are overmastered surely—if accepted
Justice still has place in the laws of god.°

    Now go! For I abominate and disown you,
wretched scum! Go with the malediction
I here pronounce for you: that you shall never   1385
master your native land by force of arms,
nor ever see your home again in Argos,

the land below the hills; but you shall die
by your own brother's hand, and you shall kill
the brother who banished you. For this I pray.
And I cry out to the hated underworld
that it may take you home; cry out to these   1390
powers indwelling here; and to that power
of furious War that filled your hearts with hate!
Now you have heard me. Go: tell it to Thebes,
tell all the Thebans; tell your faithful fighting
friends what sort of honors   1395
Oedipus has divided among his sons!

CHORUS LEADER
Polynices, I find no matter for sympathy
in your directing yourself here. You may retire.

POLYNICES
Ah, what a journey! What a failure!
My poor companions! See the finish now   1400
of all we marched from Argos for! See me . . .
for I can neither speak of this to anyone
among my friends, nor lead them back again;
I must go silently to meet this doom.
O sisters—daughters of his, sisters of mine!   1405
You heard the hard curse of our father:
for god's sweet sake, if father's curse comes true,
and if you find some way to return home,
do not, at least, dishonor me in death!
But give me a grave and what will quiet me.°   1410
Then you shall have, besides the praise he now
gives you for serving him, an equal praise
for offices you shall have paid my ghost.

ANTIGONE
Polynices, I beseech you, listen to me!

POLYNICES
Dearest—what is it? Tell me, Antigone.   1415

ANTIGONE

Withdraw your troops to Argos as soon as you can.
Do not go to your own death and your city's!

POLYNICES

But that is impossible. How could I command
that army, even backward, once I faltered?

ANTIGONE

Now why, boy, must your anger rise again?   1420
What is the good of laying waste your homeland?

POLYNICES

It is shameful to run; and it is also shameful
to be a laughingstock to a younger brother.

ANTIGONE

But see how you fulfill his prophecies!
Did he not cry that you should kill each other?   1425

POLYNICES

He wishes that. But I cannot give way.

ANTIGONE

Ah, I am desolate! But who will dare
go with you, after hearing the prophecies?

POLYNICES

I'll not report this trifle. A good commander
tells heartening news, or keeps the news to himself.   1430

ANTIGONE

Then you have made up your mind to this, my brother?

POLYNICES

Yes. And do not try to hold me back.
The dark road is before me; I must take it,
doomed by my father and his avenging Furies.
God bless you if you do what I have asked!   1435
It is only in death that you can help me now.°

Now let me go. Good-bye! You will not ever
look in my eyes again.

ANTIGONE
                      You break my heart!

POLYNICES
Do not grieve for me.

ANTIGONE
                      Who would not grieve for you,
sweet brother! You go with open eyes to death.   1440

POLYNICES
Death, if that must be.

ANTIGONE
                      No! Do as I ask!

POLYNICES
You ask the impossible.

ANTIGONE
                      Then I am lost,
if I must be deprived of you!

POLYNICES
                              All that
rests with the powers that are over us,
whether it must be so or otherwise.
You two—I pray no evil comes to you;   1445
for all men know you merit no more pain.

                              (*Exit Polynices to the side.*)

CHORUS [*singing, while Oedipus and Antigone speak in response*]
                    STROPHE A
So in this new event we see
new forms of terror working through the blind,
or else inscrutable destiny.   1450
I am not one to say "This is in vain"

of anything allotted to mankind.
Though some must fall, or fall to rise again,
time watches all things steadily—   1455

                (A terrific peal of thunder is heard.)

Ah, Zeus! Heaven's height has cracked!

                (Thunder and lightning.)

OEDIPUS

O children, children! Could someone here—
could someone bring the hero, Theseus?

ANTIGONE

Father, what is your reason for calling him?

OEDIPUS

Zeus' beating thunder, any moment now,   1460
will clap me underground: send for him quickly!

                (Thunder and lightning.)

CHORUS

        ANTISTROPHE A
Hear it° cascading down the air!
The god-thrown, the gigantic, holy sound!
Terror crawls to the tips of my hair!   1465
My heart shakes!
        There the lightning flames again!
What heavenly marvel is it bringing 'round?
I fear it, for it never comes in vain.
But for man's luck or his despair . . .°   1470

                (Another thunderclap.)

        STROPHE B
Hear the wild thunder fall!°
Towering Nature is transfixed.
Be merciful, great spirit, if you run   1480
this sword of darkness through our mother land;

come not for our confusion,°
and deal no blows to me,
though your tireless Furies stand
by him whom I have looked upon.
Great Zeus, I make my prayer to you!   1485

OEDIPUS

Is the king near by? Will he come in time
to find me still alive, my mind still clear?

ANTIGONE

Tell me what it is you have in mind!

OEDIPUS

To give him now, in return for his great kindness,
the blessing that I promised I would give.   1490

CHORUS

ANTISTROPHE B

O noble son, return!
No matter if you still descend
in the deep fastness of the sea god's grove,
to make pure offering at his altar fire: 1495
receive from this strange man
whatever may be his heart's desire
that you and I and Athens are worthy of.°
My lord, come quickly as you can!

(Enter Theseus from the side.)

THESEUS

Now why do you all together
set up this shout once more?   1500
I see it comes from you, as from our friend.
Is it a lightning bolt from Zeus? a squall
of rattling hail? Those are familiar things
when such a tempest rages over heaven.

OEDIPUS

My lord, I longed for you to come! This is   1505
gods' work, your lucky coming.

THESEUS

                    Now, what new
circumstance has arisen, son of Laius?

OEDIPUS

My life sinks in the scale: I would not die
without fulfilling what I promised Athens.

THESEUS

What proof have you that your hour has come?°   1510

OEDIPUS

The great, incessant thunder and continuous
flashes of lightning from the hand of Zeus.   1515

THESEUS

I believe you. I have seen you prophesy
many things, none falsely. What must be done?

OEDIPUS

I shall disclose to you, O son of Aegeus,
what is appointed for you and for your city:
a thing that age will never wear away.
Presently now, without a soul to guide me,   1520
I'll lead you to the place where I must die;
but you must never tell it to any man,
not even the neighborhood in which it lies.
If you obey, this will count more for you
than many shields and many neighbors' spears.   1525
These things are mysteries, not to be explained;
but you will understand when you come there
alone. Alone, because I cannot disclose it
to any of your men or to my children,
much as I love and cherish them. But you

keep it secret always, and when you come   1530
to the end of life, then you must hand it on
to your most cherished son, and he in turn
must teach it to his heir, and so forever.°
That way you shall forever hold this city
safe from the men of Thebes, the dragon's sons.

    For every nation that lives peaceably,
there will be many others to grow hard
and push their arrogance to extremes. The gods   1535
attend to these things slowly; but they attend
to those who put off god and turn to madness!
You have no mind for that, child of Aegeus.

    Indeed, you know already all that I teach.
Let us now proceed to that place   1540
and hesitate no longer; I am driven
by an insistent voice that comes from god.
Children, follow me this way: see, now,
I have become your guide, as you were mine!
Come: do not touch me: let me alone discover
the holy and funereal ground where I   1545
must take this fated earth to be my shroud.
This way, O come! The angel of the dead,
Hermes, and veiled Persephone lead me on!

       (Oedipus begins to walk to the side, leading his daughters.)

O sunlight of no light! Once you were mine!
This is the last my flesh will feel of you;   1550
for now I go to shade my ending day
in the dark underworld. Most cherished friend!
I pray that you and this your land and all
your people may be blessed: remember me.
Be mindful of my death, and be
fortunate in all the time to come!   1555

       (Exit Oedipus to the side, followed by his daughters
              and by Theseus with his soldiers.)

CHORUS [*singing*]

If I may dare to adore that lady
the living never see,
and pray to the master of spirits plunged in night,
who of vast Hell has sovereignty:°   1560
let not our friend go down in grief and weariness
to that all-shrouding fold,
the dead man's plain, the house that has no light.
Because his sufferings were great, unmerited and untold,   1565
let some just god relieve him from distress!

O powers under the earth, and tameless
beast in the passageway,
rumbler prone at the gate of the strange hosts,°   1570
their guard forever, as the legends say:
I pray you, even Death, offspring of Earth and Hell,
to let the descent be clear   1575
as Oedipus goes down among the ghosts
on those dim fields of underground that all men living fear.
Eternal sleep, let Oedipus sleep well!

(Enter a Messenger, from the side.)

MESSENGER
Citizens, the briefest way to tell you
would be to say that Oedipus is no more;   1580
but what has happened cannot be told so simply—
it was no simple thing.

CHORUS LEADER
                 He is gone, poor man?

MESSENGER
You may be sure that he has left this world.

CHORUS LEADER
By god's mercy, was his death a painless one?   1585

[215] OEDIPUS AT COLONUS

That is the thing that seems so marvelous.
You know, for you were witnesses, how he
left this place with no friend leading him,
acting, himself, as guide for all of us.
Well, when he came to the steep place in the road,   1590
the embankment there, secured with steps of brass,
he stopped in one of the many branching paths.
This was not far from the stone bowl that marks
Theseus' and Pirithous' covenant.
Halfway between that place of stone   1595
with its hollow pear tree, and the marble tomb,
he sat down and undid his filthy garments;
then he called his daughters and commanded
that they should bring him water from a fountain
for bathing and libation to the dead.
From there they saw the hillcrest of Demeter,   1600
freshener of all things: they ascended it
and soon came back with water for their father;
then helped him properly to bathe and dress.
When everything was finished to his pleasure
and no command of his remained undone,   1605
then the earth groaned with thunder from the god below;
and as they heard the sound, the girls shuddered
and dropped to their father's knees, and began wailing,
beating their breasts and weeping, as if heartbroken.
And hearing them cry out so bitterly   1610
he put his arms around them, and said to them:
"Children, this day your father is gone from you.
All that was mine is gone. You shall no longer
bear the burden of taking care of me—
I know it was hard, my children. And yet one word
frees us of all the weight and pain of life:°   1615
that word is love. You never shall have more
from anyone than you have had from me.

And now you must spend the rest of life without me."
    That was the way of it. They clung together   1620
and wept, all three. But when they finally stopped
and no more sobs were heard, then there was
silence, and in the silence suddenly
a voice cried out to him—of such a kind
it made our hair stand up in panic fear: 1625
again and again the call came from the god:
"Oedipus! Oedipus! Why are we waiting?
You delay too long; you delay too long to go!"
Then, knowing himself summoned by the spirit,
he asked that the lord Theseus come to him;   1630
and when he had come, said: "O my prince and friend,
give your right hand now as a binding pledge
to my two daughters; children, give him your hands.
Promise that you will never willingly
betray them, but will carry out in kindness
whatever is best for them in the days to come."   1635
And Theseus swore to do it for his friend,
with such restraint as fits a noble king.
And when he had done so, Oedipus at once
laid his blind hands upon his daughters, saying:
"Children, you must show your nobility,°   1640
and have the courage now to leave this spot.
You must not wish to see what is forbidden
or hear such voices as may not be heard.
But go—go quickly. Only the lord Theseus
may stay to see the thing that now begins."
    This much every one of us heard him say,   1645
and then we came away, sobbing, with the girls.
But after a little while as we withdrew
we turned around—and nowhere saw that man,
but only the king, his hands before his face,
shading his eyes as if from something fearful,   1650
awesome and unendurable to see.

Then very quickly we saw him do reverence
to Earth and to the powers of the air,
with one address to both.

But in what manner   1655
Oedipus perished, no one of mortal men
could tell but Theseus. It was not lightning,
bearing its fire from Zeus, that took him off;
no hurricane was blowing.   1660
But some attendant from the train of heaven°
came for him; or else the underworld
opened in love the unlit door of earth.
For he was taken without lamentation,
illness, or suffering; indeed his end
was wonderful if mortal's ever was.   1665
Should someone think I speak intemperately,
I make no apology to him who thinks so.

CHORUS LEADER
But where are his children and the others with them?

MESSENGER
They are not far away; the sound of weeping
should tell you now that they are coming here.

(Enter Antigone and Ismene together, from the side.)

ANTIGONE [singing in turn with Ismene and the Chorus]
STROPHE A
Now we may weep, indeed.   1670
Now, if ever, we may cry
in bitter grief against our fate,
our heritage still unappeased.
In other days we stood up under it,
endured it for his sake,
the unrelenting horror. Now the finish
comes, and we know only
in all that we have seen and done   1675
bewildering mystery.

CHORUS

   What happened?

ANTIGONE

             We can only guess, my friends.

CHORUS

   He has gone?

ANTIGONE

             He has; as one could wish him to.
   Why not? It was not war
   nor the deep sea that overtook him,   1680
   but something invisible and strange
   caught him up—or down—
   into a space unseen.
   But we are lost, dear sister. A deathly
   night is ahead of us.
   For how, in some far country wandering,   1685
   or on the lifting seas,
   shall we eke out our lives?

ISMENE

   I cannot guess. But as for me,
   I wish that murderous Hades would take me   1690
   in one death with our father.
   This is such desolation
   I cannot go on living.

CHORUS

   Most admirable sisters:
   whatever god has brought about
   is to be borne with courage.
   You must not feed the flames of grief;   1695
   no blame can come to you.

ANTIGONE

          ANTISTROPHE A
   One may long for the past

though at the time indeed it seemed
nothing but wretchedness and evil.
Life was not sweet, yet I found it so
when I could put my arms around my father.
O father! O my dear!   1700
Now you are shrouded in eternal darkness.
Even in that absence
you shall not lack our love,
mine and my sister's love.

CHORUS
He lived his life . . .

ANTIGONE
                        He did as he had wished!

CHORUS
What do you mean?   1705

ANTIGONE
                        In this land among strangers
he died where he chose to die.
He has his eternal bed well shaded
and in his death is not unmourned.
My eyes are blind with tears
from crying for you, father.   1710
The terror and the loss
cannot be quieted.
I know you wished to die in a strange country,
yet your death was so lonely!
Why could I not be with you?

ISMENE
O pity! What is left for me?   1715
What destiny awaits us both
now we have lost our father?°

CHORUS
Dear children, remember   1720

that his last hour was free and blessed.
So make an end of grieving!
Is anyone in all the world
safe from unhappiness?

ANTIGONE

STROPHE B

Let us run back there!

ISMENE

Why, what shall we do?

ANTIGONE

I am carried away with longing—   1725

ISMENE

For what—tell me!

ANTIGONE

To see the resting place in the earth—

ISMENE

Of whom?

ANTIGONE

Father's! O, what misery I feel!

ISMENE

But that is not permitted. Do you not see?   1730

ANTIGONE

Do not rebuke me!

ISMENE

And remember, too—

ANTIGONE

Oh, what?

ISMENE

He had no tomb; there was no one near!

ANTIGONE

Take me there and you can kill me, too!

ISMENE
    Ah! I am truly lost!
    Helpless and so forsaken!   1735
    Where shall I go and how shall I live?

CHORUS

ANTISTROPHE B

    You must not fear, now.

ANTIGONE
                 Yes, but where is a refuge?

CHORUS
    A refuge has been found —

ANTIGONE
               Where do you mean?

CHORUS
    A place where you will be unharmed!   1740

ANTIGONE
                    No . . .

CHORUS
    What are you thinking?

ANTIGONE
             I think there is no way
    for me to get home again.

CHORUS
             Do not go home!

ANTIGONE
    My home is in trouble.

CHORUS
            So it has been before.

ANTIGONE
    There was no help for it then: but now it is worse.   1745

CHORUS

A wide and desolate world it is for you.°

ANTIGONE

Great god! What way is there, O Zeus?
Do the powers that rule our lives
still press me on to hope at all?   1750

(Enter Theseus from the side, with attendants.)

THESEUS° [chanting in alternation with Antigone and the Chorus until
the end of the play]

Mourn no more, children. Those to whom
the night of earth gives benediction
should not be mourned. Retribution comes.

ANTIGONE

Theseus: we fall on our knees to you!

THESEUS

What is it that you desire, children?   1755

ANTIGONE

We wish to see the place ourselves
in which our father rests.

THESEUS

No, no.
It is not permissible to go there.

ANTIGONE

My lord and ruler of Athens, why?

THESEUS

Because your father told me, children,   1760
that no one should go near the spot.
No mortal man should tell of it,
since it is holy, and is his.
And if I kept this pledge, he said,
I should preserve my land from its enemies.   1765

I swore I would, and the god heard me,
the oathkeeper who makes note of all.°

ANTIGONE

If this was our father's cherished wish,
we must be satisfied.
Send us back, then, to ancient Thebes,   1770
in hopes we may stop the bloody war
from coming between our brothers!

THESEUS

I will do that, and whatever else
I am able to do for your happiness,
for his sake who has gone just now   1775
beneath the earth. I must not fail.

CHORUS

Now let the weeping cease;
let no one mourn again.
These things are in the hands of god.°

TEXTUAL NOTES

(Line numbers are in some cases only approximate.)

ANTIGONE

5. Text uncertain.

45. Exact text and interpretation uncertain.

572–76. The assignment of speakers in lines 572, 574, and 576 varies among the manuscripts, early printed editions, and modern editors. Some assign 572 and 574 to Antigone; some assign all three lines (572, 574, 576) to Ismene.

602. Text uncertain: "knife" (*kopis*) is a modern emendation; the manuscripts have "dust" (*konis*).

606. The exact text and sense are uncertain.

781. Possibly Creon does not go inside now but remains onstage for the chorus's song, which would be unusual but not unprecedented in Greek tragedy.

782. Text and interpretation uncertain.

882. Possibly Creon has been present onstage throughout the lyric scene that preceded: see note on 781.

882–84. Text and precise meaning uncertain.

978. Exact text and interpretation not certain.

1080–83. Some editors delete these lines, in the belief that they were added (by someone other than Sophocles) so as to remind the audience of the story of the "Successors of the Seven" (*Epigoni*). Other editors retain the lines, but suggest that a few additional lines of explanation may have dropped out between 1080 and 1081.

1301. Text and interpretation uncertain; it appears that a line is missing here as well.

81. Text uncertain: possibly "be happy like his eyes, and bring us safety."

198. Text uncertain.

246-51. Some editors reject these lines, regarding them as redundant after 236-43.

293. This emendation is widely accepted for the manuscript reading "No one sees who saw it."

420-21. The precise reading and interpretation are uncertain.

425. This is the reading of the manuscripts. Some editors emend the text to read, "other evils / annihilating you together with your children."

479. Or possibly "limping on his feet."

566. This is a widely accepted emendation of the manuscript reading, which has "search for the dead man."

600. This line is deleted by some scholars as an interpolation.

623-27. Two or three lines appear to have dropped out here, as the sequence of dialogue is unsatisfactory and the sense unclear.

641. The precise reading is uncertain here.

1205. The reading and interpretation here are quite uncertain, though the general sense is clear.

1280. The precise reading here is uncertain.

1316. Text and translation uncertain.

1349-50. Some editors adopt an emendation which gives, "Curse on the shepherd who . . ."

1522-30. Some editors have rejected all these final lines, arguing that they are not written in proper Sophoclean style.

OEDIPUS AT COLONUS

3. More exactly, "this day."

8. More accurately, "nobility."

49-50. Or more literally, "By the gods, stranger, do not dishonor a wanderer such as I am, by refusing to tell me what I ask."

95. More exactly, "the bright flash of Zeus."

97. Or, "with trustworthy omens."

103. More exactly, "according to the sacred utterances of Apollo."

127–28. More literally, "into the inviolate grove of these dreadful Maidens," that is, the Furies.

164. Some editors emend to read "Let there be a greater distance from there."

171. More exactly, "Father, we should pay attention to the townsmen."

183. About four lyric lines appear to be missing before this, since the corresponding antistrophe has several more phrases than the strophe here.

212. More exactly, "My birth and nature are dreadful."

235–37. Or more exactly, "Depart quickly from my land, lest you bring some further trouble to my city!"

248. More literally, "Grant your unexpected approval!"

253. More accurately, "You will never see a mortal man who, if a god leads, can escape."

279–80. More exactly, "upon the mortal who is reverent, and upon the irreverent too."

287–90. More accurately, "I come here sacred and reverent, and I bring advantage to this race, as you may learn more fully when the man with authority comes, whoever is your leader."

325. Or "sweetest names to utter!"

327. Text uncertain: the manuscripts have "unfortunate," but the emendation "old and worn" is preferred by many editors.

371. More exactly, "some god" and "their own evil/sinful mind."

378. More exactly, "has gone to Argos . . . as an exile."

380–81. The text is uncertain here. Many editors adopt a simple emendation, so that instead of "Argos shall . . . win . . . ," Polynices is telling them that "he himself shall . . . win Thebes . . . or else go up to heaven."

406. More exactly, "Will they cover my body with Theban dust?"

450. More exactly, "They will never win me as their ally."

508-9. More literally, "For parents, not even if one labors should it be thought of as labor."

527-28. More exactly, "Was it with your mother, as I hear, that you shared your ill-famed bed?"

539-40. More literally, "I received a gift, which I wish I had never accepted, for having given help."

547. Text uncertain. Some editors emend to read "I was captured by doom; I killed . . ."

579. More accurately, "What profit do you claim to bring?"

587. More exactly, "The contest is no small one."

590. More accurately, "But if you wish that, it is not good for you to remain in exile."

606. More literally, "And how would my affairs and theirs become bitter?"

658-60. Many scholars have rejected these lines as a post-Sophoclean interpolation.

669-71. More exactly, "*you have come, guest, to Colonus . . . and you shall not seek another home.*"

685-87. More literally, "*the river's fountains are awake, Cephisus' nomadic streams that run unthinned forever, and never stay . . .*"

695-98. More precisely, "*And our land has a thing unknown in Asia's vast terrain or in the Dorian isle to our west where Pelops' race holds sway.*"

718-19. Or, a little more exactly, "*following the hundred-footed Nereids and their dance.*"

735-36. More exactly, "I, despite my age, am sent to persuade him to follow me back to Thebes."

756-57. Text uncertain.

848. Literally, "Oh wretched, wretched am I!"

861-62. In the manuscripts, both these lines are spoken by Creon, and the reading is "It will be done, unless the ruler of this land prevents me!" Several modern editors have emended the second line so as to read "you," as here, and have assigned this line to the chorus.

882. A few words in the chorus' reply seem to be missing here.

942. More literally, "my relatives."

945. The reading is uncertain. The text in the manuscripts seems to refer to "someone with whom children from an unholy marriage are living."

954-55. Some editors regard these two lines as an interpolation.

964-65. More exactly, "It was the gods' pleasure, and perhaps our family had angered them long ago."

975-76. More exactly, "and killed him, not knowing what I was doing, nor whom I was doing it to."

1007-8. More literally, "me, an old man and a suppliant ..."

1033. Some editors transpose lines 1028-33 to follow 1019.

1043. More literally, "and may you benefit from your righteous concern for us!"

1044-95. Robert Fitzgerald's version of this choral song is composed as a sequence of rhyming stanzas and refrains, and it is somewhat freer as a translation of Sophocles' Greek than his rendering of the other choral songs of the play. A less poetic, but more exact, version of the first strophe and antistrophe might be the following:

STROPHE A

Oh, to be where the enemies wheel about,
to hear the shout and brazen sound of war!   1045
Or maybe on Apollo's sacred shore,
or by that torchlit Eleusinian plain
where pilgrims come, so that
the Great Ladies may provide solemn rites
for those mortals on whose tongues the golden key   1050
of the sweet-voiced Ministers rests.
For even to those regions the warrior king Theseus
will press the fighting on—as he brings
help to the two maiden sisters,   1055
self-sufficient in his battle-strength!

ANTISTROPHE A

Perhaps they are approaching now the plain
west of snowy mount Oea,   1060
if they are fleeing on horses
or on swift-racing chariots;
yet they'll be taken: for fearsome is the spirit   1065

of the local people, and fearsome Theseus's army;
the harnesses flash like mountain lightning.
These are the riders of Athens, conquered never;
they honor her whose glory all men know,   1070
and honor Poseidon too, son of Rhea and god of the sea,
the one who holds the earth firm.

1067–69. Text uncertain.

1080. More exactly, "I can prophesy a good outcome to this contest!"

1094–95. More exactly, "so that both of you come to lend your help to this land and its citizens."

1116. More accurately, "for girls so young."

1118. The precise text is uncertain here, but the general sense seems clear.

1158. More literally, "sitting as a suppliant at Poseidon's altar."

1166. More exactly, "would come here to make this supplication?"

1202–3. Or, more exactly, "and you, who are yourself being well treated, should know how to pay proper return for such treatment."

1210. More exactly, "you are safe, if one of the gods will keep my life safe too."

1268. More exactly, "of Zeus."

1278. More literally, "I am a suppliant of the god."

1300. This line is rejected by some editors as an interpolation.

1341. More literally, "scattering him."

1357. More exactly, "clad in these rags that now you are weeping about."

1370. More exactly, "And so it is that a god is watching you."

1373. Literally, "polluted by blood."

1382. More accurately, "of Zeus."

1410. More literally, "proper funeral rites."

1436. Some editors reject this line as an interpolation.

1463. More exactly, "Look there!"

1470. After this line, the manuscripts contain several more lines, which Robert Fitzgerald originally translated as follows:

CHORUS [*singing*]
Ah, Zeus! Majestic heaven!

OEDIPUS
My children, the appointed end has come;
I can no longer turn away from it.

ANTIGONE
How do you know? What is the sign that tells you?

OEDIPUS
I know it clearly now. Let someone quickly   1475
send for the king and bring him here to me!

(Thunder and lightning.)

1477. In the manuscripts, this choral stanza begins, "*Ah, ah, see once more!*"

1482–84. Or more exactly:

May I find you favorably disposed,
and though I have looked on an accursed man,
may I not be paid back to my loss!

1498. More exactly, "*as just repayment to you and the city and his dear ones for what he has endured.*"

1511–13. The manuscripts here contain three lines which Robert Fitzgerald does not translate:

OEDIPUS
The gods themselves as heralds proclaim to me
with no deception; the signs are plain and true.

THESEUS
What do you mean? How are these things revealed?

1531–32. More literally:

then you must tell it
only to the foremost citizen, and he in turn
must teach it to his successor, and so forever.

1559–60. More literally, "*pray to you, Aidoneus, king of the regions of night.*"

1570. More exactly, "*the invincible beast Cerberus, growling at the gate of the all-welcoming hosts.*"

1615. More literally, "And yet one word dissolves all those hardships."

1640. The exact text is uncertain but the meaning is clear.

1661. More exactly, "But either some escort sent from the gods . . ."

1717. Some words have apparently dropped out here, since the antistrophe is two lines shorter than the corresponding strophe.

1746. More literally, "*A wide sea of troubles it is for you.*" This line is followed in the manuscripts by Antigone singing "Yes, yes" and the chorus "I agree too." Some scholars reject these phrases as an interpolation.

1751-53. The manuscripts attribute these lines to the Chorus Leader, but modern scholars assign them to Theseus.

1767. More exactly, "*and the god heard me, and so did Oath, the son of Zeus, who hears everything.*"

1779. More literally, "*Altogether, these things have their appointed end.*"

GLOSSARY

Abae: town in northeastern Phocis famous for its oracle of Apollo.
Acheron: river or lake in the underworld across which the dead are ferried.
Adrastus: king of Argos; father of Argeia, wife of Polyneices.
Aegeus: king of Athens; father of Theseus.
Aetolia: region in Greece north of the Gulf of Corinth, west of Phocis.
Agenor: father of Cadmus and Europa.
Aidoneus: another form of the name Hades.
Amphiaraus: seer and warrior from Argos; one of the Seven, who fought against Thebes.
Amphion: cofounder of Thebes (with his twin brother Zethus); built the city's walls by moving the stones with his lyre; husband of Niobe, Tantalus' daughter.
Amphitrite: wife of Poseidon.
Antigone: daughter of Oedipus and Jocasta; sister of Ismene, Polyneices, and Eteocles.
Apollo: son of Zeus and Leto; twin brother of Artemis; born on Delos; god of prophecy, poetry, archery, and healing. His main prophetic seat is at Delphi. *See also* Loxias; Pythian
Apollo's sacred strand: the pass at Daphne, about six miles west of Colonus.
Arcadia: a region in the center of the Peloponnesus.
Areopagus: "Hill of Ares"; the hill in Athens near the Acropolis where the ancient Council met to hold homicide trials.
Ares: god of war; son of Zeus and Hera; father of Harmonia, Cadmus' wife.
Argive: of Argos.
Argos: city in the Peloponnesus located in the southern region of the Argive plain.
Artemis: daughter of Zeus and Leto; twin sister of Apollo; born on Delos; associated especially with childhood, wild animals, hunting, and childbirth.
Asia: Asia "Minor," i.e., Anatolia (modern-day Turkey).

Atalanta: mother of Parthenopaeus; took part in the Calydonian boar hunt.

Athena: daughter of Zeus (and Metis); goddess of wisdom and war; patron goddess of Athens.

Athens: main city in the plain of Attica in Greece.

Attica: peninsula, to the southeast of Boeotia, extending into the Aegean Sea; Athens is its chief city.

Bacchants: followers of Bacchus, usually female.

Bacchus, Bacchic god: see Dionysus

Bosporus (or Bosphorus): sometimes used as another name for the Hellespont, the strait connecting Anatolia (modern-day Turkey) and Greece. The true Bosphorus, however, was the strait dividing Europe from Asia at Byzantium/Chalcedon (modern-day Istanbul).

Cadmus: son of Agenor; brother of Europa; father of Semele, Agave, Autonoë, Ino, and Polydorus; first founder of Thebes.

Capaneus: one of the Seven (with Polyneices), who fought against Thebes.

Castalia: nymph who gives her name to the spring at the foot of Mount Parnassus.

Cephisus: the name of several rivers in Greece, including one on Mount Parnassus (Boeotia) and another in Attica, near Athens.

Cerberus: the monstrous, three-headed dog that guards entry to the underworld.

Cithaeron: mountain in central Greece near Thebes on which Oedipus was abandoned; Boeotia is to its north, Attica to its south.

Cleopatra: wife of Phineus.

Colonus: legendary horseman and eponymous hero of the deme of Colonus, a district of Athens located about one mile northwest of the center of the city.

Corinth: Isthmus that connects the Peloponnesus to central Greece.

Creon: son of Menoeceus; brother of Jocasta; became king of Thebes twice, first after Oedipus' fall, then after Eteocles' death.

Cronus: king of the Titans; father of Zeus, Poseidon, and the other Olympian gods.

Cyllene: mountain in northeastern Arcadia on which Hermes was born (thus the title "Cyllene's king").

Danaë: daughter of Acrisius, who, when warned that her son would kill him, imprisoned her in a tower to keep her from becoming pregnant. Zeus visited her in the form of a golden shower and she duly gave birth to Perseus.

Daulia: a town in Phocis or Boeotia, about fifteen miles northeast of Delphi.

Death: see Hades; Pluto

Delian Healer: see Apollo, whose birthplace was the island of Delos.

Delphi: town on the southwestern slope of Mount Parnassus in Phocis; the site of the Delphic oracle, sacred to Apollo.

Demeter: sister of Zeus and one of the twelve Olympian gods; mother of Persephone. She and her daughter are celebrated especially at Eleusis, a town in Attica about twelve miles northwest of Athens.

Dionysus: son of Zeus and Semele; god of theater, liberation, and wine; also known as Bacchus.

Dirce's stream/spring: a river to the west of Thebes.

Doorsill of Brass: point of entry to the underworld.

Dorian (Dorians): the inhabitants of the Peloponnesus (*see* Pelops); so "Dorian isle" can refer to the Peloponnesus.

Dorian land: used here specifically of Argos.

Dryas: father of Lycurgus, the Thracian king who, maddened by Dionysus for imprisoning his maenads, mistook his own son for a trunk of ivy and pruned him to death.

Eleusis, Eleusinian shore: Eleusis is a town about twelve miles northwest of Athens, famous for its annual festival of the Mysteries. *See also* Demeter

Erechthids: descendants of Erechtheus, a legendary early king of Athens.

Eteocles: son and brother of Oedipus; son of Jocasta; brother of Antigone, Ismene, and Polyneices; defended Thebes against his brother's attack with the Seven.

Eteoclus: one of the Seven who fought against Thebes.

Euboea: the long island east of Boeotia.

Eumenides: a euphemism for the Furies or August Goddesses (*Semnai Theai*); the name means "Kindly Ones."

Eurydice: wife of Creon; mother of Haemon (and of Megareus).

Fortune: in Greek, *Tychê*; sometimes imagined as a female divinity.

Fury, Furies: female avenging spirit(s) (Greek *erinys*), especially concerned with bloodguilt. *See also* Eumenides

Gentle All-Seeing Ones: *see* Eumenides

Hades: god of and the name for the underworld; brother of Zeus and Poseidon; husband of Persephone.

Haemon: son of Creon and Eurydice; fiancé of Antigone.

Hell: either Tartarus (the lowest region of the underworld), or the underworld in general.

Hellas: Greece.

Hermes: son of Zeus and Maia; god of travelers, contests, stealth, trade, and heralds; he escorts dead souls to Hades.

Hippomedon: son of Talaus; one of the Seven, who fought against Thebes.

Iacchus: another name for Bacchus/Dionysus.

Ismene: sister of Antigone, Polyneices, and Eteocles; sister and daughter of
Oedipus; daughter of Jocasta.

Ismenus: river which flows from the foothills of Mount Cithaeron past
Thebes.

Ister: river (modern-day Danube), which flows from central Europe into the
Black Sea.

Isthmus: the narrow strip of land connecting the Peloponnesus in southern
Greece to the mainland.

Italy's master: (here) Dionysus.

Jocasta: daughter of Menoeceus; sister of Creon; wife of Laius; mother and
wife of Oedipus; mother of Antigone, Ismene, Eteocles, and Polyneices.

Justice: in Greek, *Dikê*; sometimes personified as daughter of Zeus.

Labdacids, Labdacidae: descendants of Labdacus, i.e., the Theban royal
family.

Labdacus: son of Polydorus; father of Laius.

Laius: son of Labdacus; king of Thebes; husband of Jocasta; father of
Oedipus.

Loxias: epithet of Apollo often used in place of his name; the name means
"crooked" and may come from the riddling nature of Apollo's oracles.

Lycian (Lycian king): epithet of Apollo because he was worshipped on
Mount Lycaeum in Arcadia.

Lydia (Lydian): a region in western Anatolia (modern-day Turkey). Its chief
city was Sardis.

maenad: female follower of Dionysus. *See also* Bacchants

Megareus: son of Creon and Eurydice, apparently killed (sacrificed?) during
the course of the battle against the Seven. (In other versions he is called
Menoeceus.)

Menoeceus: the name of Creon's father and of his son (though his son is
sometimes called Megareus instead).

Merope: wife of Polybus of Corinth; adoptive mother of Oedipus.

Ministers: the aristocratic family of the Eumolpids (whose name means
"good singers"), who presided over the Eleusinian Mysteries.

Nereids: fifty daughters of the sea-god Nereus; sea-nymphs.

nymphs: minor female divinities variously associated with almost all
aspects of nature (trees, fountains, mountains, the sea, etc.).

Oea: mountain in Attica.

Oedipus: son of Laius; son and husband of Jocasta; father and brother of
Antigone, Ismene, Eteocles, and Polyneices; king of Thebes.

Oeneus: father of Tydeus; king of Calydon.

Olympia: sanctuary of Zeus in Elis (western Peloponnesus) with an oracle
of Zeus.

Olympian: of Olympus (often applied to Zeus in particular).

Olympus: mountain on which the gods make their home, located in Pieria in northern Greece.

Pallas: Athena.

Pan: a god of flocks and shepherds, at home in woodlands and on mountainsides.

Parnassus: mountain in central Greece which towers over Delphi.

Parthenopaeus: Arcadian hero who was one of the Seven who fought against Thebes; son of Atalanta.

Pegasus: winged horse born from the Gorgon Medusa's neck after she was decapitated by Perseus.

Peloponnesus: the large area of southern Greece, connected to the rest by the Isthmus of Corinth.

Pelops: son of Tantalus; legendary founder of the Peloponnesus ("Isle of Pelops"). *See also* Dorian isle

Persephone: daughter of Zeus and Demeter; wife of Hades; queen of the underworld. *See also* Eleusis

Phasis: river (modern-day Rion[i]), which flows from the Caucasus Mountains into the Black Sea.

Phineus: king of Salmydessus; husband of Cleopatra, with whom he had two sons. He imprisoned her and remarried. His new wife, Eidothea, blinded his two sons.

Phocis: a region in central Greece. *See also* Delphi

Phoebus: an epithet of Apollo meaning "bright."

Phrygia, Phrygian: a region in northwest Anatolia (modern-day Turkey).

Pirithous: king of the Lapiths; husband of Hippodameia. He helped Theseus in his attempt to abduct Persephone from the underworld.

Pluto: king of the underworld; sometimes identified with Hades.

Polybus: husband of Merope; king of Corinth; adoptive father of Oedipus.

Polydorus: son of Cadmus and Harmonia; father of Labdacus.

Polyneices, or Polynices: son of Oedipus and Jocasta; brother of Eteocles, Ismene, and Antigone; married Argeia, daughter of Adrastus, king of Argos, and waged war on Thebes as one of the Seven.

Poseidon: brother of Zeus; one of the twelve Olympian gods; god of the sea, of earthquakes, and of horses; father of Theseus.

Prometheus: a Titan; son of Iapetus; stole fire from the gods and gave it to mankind, for which he was punished by Zeus.

Pytho, Pythian: another name for Delphi; the name Pytho comes from the serpent Python whom Apollo slew.

Rhea: wife of Cronus; mother of Zeus, Poseidon, and the other Olympian gods.

Salmydessus: city in Thrace on the west coast of the Black Sea, about sixty
miles northwest from the Hellespont.

Semele: daughter of Cadmus and Harmonia; sister of Agave, Autonoë, and
Ino; mother of Dionysus, with Zeus.

Sicilian: of Sicily, an island on the tip of the "boot" of Italy famous for its
horses.

Sipylus: a city in Phrygia or Lydia; home of King Tantalus and his daughter,
Niobe.

Sphinx: mythological monster with the head of woman, body of a lion, and
wings of an eagle who guarded the entrance to Thebes and asked pass-
ersby a riddle posed in poetic form. Those who failed to answer correctly
were killed.

Talaus: father of Hippomedon; one of the Argonauts.

Tantalus: king of Sipylus, in Anatolia; father of Niobe; she boasted that
because she and her husband Amphion had fourteen children (the number varies) she was better than Leto, who had only two: Apollo and Artemis. As punishment for such a boast, Apollo and Artemis killed Niobe's
children; Niobe never ceased mourning and turned to stone.

Teiresias: blind Theban seer of Apollo.

Thebes (or Thebe), Thebans: city in Boeotia fifty miles northwest of Athens,
and its people.

Theseus: son of Aegeus (or Poseidon); mythical king of Athens, and the
Athenians' most popular hero; often regarded as their founding father.

Thessalian: of Thessaly, a region north of central Greece, south of Macedo-
nia, and bordering on the Aegean Sea to the east.

Thrace: extensive region to the northeast of Greece which covers what is
today northeastern Greece, southeastern Bulgaria, and northwest Turkey.

Tydeus: son of Oeneus; father of Diomedes; one of the Seven who fought
against Thebes.

war god: *see* Ares

Western God: Hades.

Zeus, Zeus Artificer: king of gods and men.